Clinician's Manual
for Preventing and Treating
Juvenile Fire Involvement

TAPP-C

Version 1.0

Sherri MacKay, PhD
Centre for Addiction and Mental Health

Joanna Henderson, PhD
Centre for Addiction and Mental Health

Carol Root, PhD
Centre for Addiction and Mental Health

Diane Warling, PhD
Centre for Addiction and Mental Health

K.B. Gilbert, M.Ed.
Office of the Fire Marshal of Ontario

Janice Johnstone
Office of the Fire Marshal of Ontario

camh
Centre for Addiction and Mental Health
Centre de toxicomanie et de santé mentale

A Pan American Health Organization /
World Health Organization
Collaborating Centre

TAPP-C: Clinician's Manual for Preventing and Treating Juvenile Fire Involvement

Version 1.0

National Library of Canada Cataloguing in Publication

TAPP-C : clinician's manual for preventing and treating juvenile fire involvement / authors, Sherri MacKay ... [et al.].

Includes bibliographical references.

ISBN 0-88868-444-4

1. Fire behavior in children—Prevention.
2. Pyromania in children—Treatment.

I. MacKay, Sherri, 1955-
II. Centre for Addiction and Mental Health
III. Title.

RJ506.P95T36 2003
618.92'85843
C2003-900617-4

Printed in Canada

For information on other Centre for Addiction and Mental Health resource materials or to place an order, please contact:

Marketing and Sales Services
Centre for Addiction and Mental Health
33 Russell Street
Toronto, Ontario
Canada M5S 2S1

Tel.: 1 800 661-1111 or 416 595-6059 in Toronto

E-mail: marketing@camh.net

Web site: www.camh.net

This manual was produced by:

Development
Margaret Kittel Canale, M.Ed., CAMH

Editorial
Diana Ballon, MSW, CAMH
Kate Baltais, MA

Design
Eva Katz, MA, CAMH
Bob Tarjan, B.A.Sc., CAMH

Print production
Christine Harris, CAPPM, CAMH

Marketing
Bernard King, MA, CAMH
Rosalicia Rondon, MBA, CAMH

This publication makes every attempt to provide accurate and authoritative information in regard to the subject matter covered. It is sold with the understanding that the publisher and authors are not engaged in rendering medical, psychological, social, financial, legal or other professional services. The contents of this publication are based on information available at the time of publication.

TAPP-C is a registered trademark of the Office of the Fire Marshal of Ontario, used by permission of the Ontario Ministry of Public Safety and Security.

Acknowledgments

The authors would like to thank the following people and agencies for their help with this treatment manual.

Special recognition and thanks for help with the development of the TAPP-C program to:

Mark Hanson, MD

Peter Marton, PhD

The authors gratefully acknowledge the ongoing financial support given to TAPP-C by:

Centre for Addiction and Mental Health (CAMH)

Fire Marshal's Public Fire Safety Council (FMPFSC)

Office of the Fire Marshal of Ontario (OFM)

Toronto Fire Services (TFS)

Helpful comments on drafts were received from:

Leena K. Augimeri, M.Ed.

Cathy Clarke, MSW

Larry Danilewitz, PhD

Linda Hall, PhD

Kathy Sdao-Jarvie, PhD

Chris Wekerle, PhD

Steven Welowszky, BPHE

And finally, sincere thanks to the many mental health and fire service colleagues, staff and students who have worked on TAPP-C over the years and to the numerous families, children and youth who participated in the program.

Contents

Part 3   Child Treatment Sessions

Part 4   Special Issues

Part 1

About the Program

TAPP-C

What is TAPP-C?

The Arson Prevention Program for Children (TAPP-C) was developed in the early 1990s as an empirically-based assessment and intervention program to address the firesetting behaviours of children and youth.

TAPP-C is a collaborative program that brings together fire service and mental health professionals to work with children, teens and their families to eliminate dangerous fire-related behaviours. Fire service professionals provide children and teens and their families with home fire-safety checks and fire-safety education, and mental health professionals conduct risk assessments and provide parent- and child-focused treatment within a mental health framework.

TAPP-C was developed as a joint venture of the Centre for Addiction and Mental Health, the Office of the Fire Marshal of Ontario and the Toronto Fire Services. Each of these organizations continues to provide TAPP-C with ongoing support.

The mental health treatment component of TAPP-C is a brief intervention program with two modules: one for parents and caregivers (who in this manual are referred to collectively as *caregivers)* and another, similar module for children and youth (who in this manual are referred to collectively as *children).*

The intervention program has been designed to specifically address firesetting and all other types of inappropriate fire involvement by children and adolescents. It uses principles of parent management training (PMT) for caregivers (Cunningham, Bremner & Boyle, 1995; Kazdin, Siegel & Bass, 1992; Webster-Stratton, Hollinsworth & Kolpacoff, 1989) and elements of cognitive behaviour therapy (CBT) for children and youth (Augimeri, Koegl & Goldberg, 2001; Kazdin, Bass, Siegel & Thomas, 1989; Kendall & Braswell, 1993; Larson & Lochman, 2002; Webster, Augimeri & Koegl, 2002).

The treatment component of TAPP-C is considered one piece of a broad range of services that may be necessary to provide to children and their caregivers in order to adequately address children's fire involvement. Ideally, prior to providing the treatment component of TAPP-C, children's firesetting risk should be evaluated using a combination of specialized firesetting risk assessment and general mental health assessment. Based on the results of these assessments, particular children may be provided with the TAPP-C treatment component in combination with more general mental health treatment; other children, whose firesetting risk is determined to be low, may receive the TAPP-C treatment as a stand-alone intervention.

Why is there a need for a brief intervention designed specifically for fire involvement?

Many of the children and adolescents who have been involved with starting fires or playing with matches or lighters also have other clinically significant difficulties (Kolko, 1996). These difficulties often include disruptive behaviour disorders, such as Attention-Deficit/Hyperactivity Disorder (ADHD), Oppositional Defiant Disorder (ODD) and Conduct Disorder (CD), as well as more general family, peer and/or academic difficulties. While these difficulties are important for treatment planning, firesetting and other types of fire involvement are important to address early in treatment for a number of reasons.

First, and most importantly, all types of fire involvement, regardless of motivation or intention, have the potential to cause significant injury or even death, not only to the child involved, but also to others in the vicinity, house or building. In addition, all types of fire involvement have the potential to cause significant property damage. Because of the associated risk of injury, caregivers, children and adolescents may be more easily motivated to address fire involvement than some of the other difficulties that may be present.

Second, fire involvement requires fire-starting materials and opportunities to engage in fire-related behaviours. These aspects of fire involvement provide specific and concrete targets for intervention that may provide greater opportunities for successful intervention than more general behavioural difficulties, such as poor peer relations.

Lastly, in many cases, fire involvement is a specific instance of a child or adolescent's broader-based behavioural difficulties. As such, it provides an opportunity for caregivers, children and adolescents to develop skills that are transferable to the management of other problems. Once learned, these skills can be used to address some of the other difficulties they may be experiencing.

What does the treatment component of TAPP-C involve?

The TAPP-C intervention approach is collaborative, involving clinicians, caregivers and children working together to address fire involvement. The role of the clinician is to help caregivers and children develop and implement their own individualized solutions to the fire involvement.

Parent management training (PMT) programs have been developed to help the parents of children with disruptive behaviour enhance their skills in reducing their children's difficult behaviours. Similar to such PMT programs, one of the goals of the treatment component of TAPP-C is to help enhance the skills of the caregivers of children with identified fire-related behaviours, in part by promoting their children's fire-safe behaviours. As well, the TAPP-C intervention addresses parental supervision and monitoring practices, reinforcing and consequencing behaviour, and planning for future difficulties within the context of the child's fire involvement.

Similar to cognitive behaviour therapy (CBT) programs that have been developed for children and adolescents with impulse control difficulties (e.g., Earlscourt Child and Family Centre, 2001a, 200lb), the TAPP-C intervention program also aims to provide children and adolescents with strategies to recognize and control their fire-related impulses and behaviours.

The treatment component of TAPP-C is derived from a social learning theoretical framework and is based on the following three principles:

1. Fire involvement by children and teens indicates an absence of fire-safe behaviours.

2. Fire-related behaviours are learned.

3. The family home—or an alternative caregiving environment—is an important setting for learning fire-safe behaviours.

The TAPP-C treatment component involves approximately five 90-minute sessions with the caregiver(s) and five 90-minute sessions with the child. The caregiver and child sessions contain some overlapping content and some content that is unique to each.

Ideally, two clinicians are available to work independently with the child and caregiver(s) for each session so that the child and caregiver modules can run concurrently. With this model, each session begins and ends with a joint meeting of the caregiver and child together with the clinicians. The purpose of the joint meetings is to enhance co-operation by jointly reviewing the core content of the session and the home practice exercises. If only one clinician is available, alternative models are possible.

Each treatment session includes:

· checking in about any further fire involvement

· reviewing information about the child's fire-specific experience related to the session topic

· psychoeducation about a target skill for that session

· in-session practice of the new skill and

· take-home exercises for skill development.

Using intervention strategies that emphasize active client participation has been found to provide greater treatment efficacy (Bloomquist & Schnell, 2002; Reid, Patterson & Snyder, 2002). Accordingly, the TAPP-C treatment component places heavy emphasis on client participation and practice. For example, clinicians are encouraged to guide participants through thoughtful questions so that participants will generate their own plans for addressing the fire involvement, identify obstacles to implementing those plans, and come up with their own potential solutions to likely barriers.

The TAPP-C treatment component includes the following topics:

· the dangerousness of fire involvement

· the importance of fire-safe attitudes

· the role of fire-safe behaviours for the family

· understanding and eliminating access to fire-starting materials and other fire-related materials

· eliminating inappropriate modelling of fire-related behaviour

· understanding high risk situations and other triggers to fire involvement

· improving supervision and monitoring practices

· developing alternative responses to triggers

· understanding the consequences of fire involvement and developing an appropriate consequence plan

· gaining support from others and

· planning for the future and monitoring for changes that may signal increased risk.

What outcomes can be expected from the treatment component of TAPP-C?

Research examining the effectiveness of PMT programs for the parents of children with disruptive behaviour difficulties indicates that these strategies can lead to substantial improvements in the children's behaviour (Cunningham, Bremner & Boyle, 1995; Kazdin, Siegel & Bass, 1992; Webster-Stratton, Hollinsworth & Kolpacoff, 1989). CBT programs for children with disruptive behaviour problems show similarly effective results (Augimeri, Koegl & Goldberg, 2001; Kazdin, Bass, Siegel & Thomas, 1989; Kendall & Braswell, 1993; Larson & Lochman, 2002; Webster, Augimeri & Koegl, 2002).

These findings hold true both when the treatments are administered individually (that is, PMT only or CBT only) as well as when they are administered in combination (PMT + CBT) (Kazdin, Siegel & Bass, 1992). However, treatment that provides a combination of PMT and CBT is more effective than either alone (Kazdin, Siegel & Bass, 1992). Accordingly, it is advised that both the TAPP-C caregiver intervention module and the child intervention module be administered.

It is also clear from the research that using a collaborative model of intervention is associated with more positive treatment outcomes in families where children are experiencing behavioural difficulties than using models where the clients have no interactive input (Webster-Stratton & Hancock, 1998).

Preliminary evaluations of TAPP-C

Preliminary evaluations of the treatment component of TAPP-C are promising. Over four years, approximately 200 families have participated in the TAPP-C research project at the Centre for Addiction and Mental Health in Toronto, Ontario, Canada. These families received:

· comprehensive risk assessments

· an earlier version of the interventions in this manual

· fire-safety education from the fire department and

· in many cases, referral for other mental health services.

Follow-up evaluations conducted with these families one year after receiving the initial services suggest that TAPP-C is as effective as firesetting treatment programs currently described in the literature (e.g., Kolko, 2001). Similar to Kolko's findings, approximately three-quarters of TAPP-C parents report no further fire involvement by their children (MacKay & Henderson, 2002).

These results, taken together with evidence for the efficacy of PMT and CBT from the research literature, provide preliminary support for the

TAPP-C treatment component as a promising intervention for a clinically-referred sample of families with children or adolescents who have engaged in firesetting or other types of fire involvement.

Future research plans include conducting a randomized, controlled treatment study using this manual, to further examine the effectiveness of the TAPP-C treatment component.

Factors that may affect success or failure of TAPP-C treatment

On the basis of the evidence from studies of therapies with children who have behavioural problems, the success of TAPP-C is likely to be affected by the following:

· whether or not the caregiver and the child attend and complete all sessions

· the extent of client participation in the session and

· the completion of home practice exercises.

Similar to other treatment programs, the effectiveness of TAPP-C will undoubtedly be affected by:

· parent factors, such as mental health issues

· child factors, such as the severity of the firesetting behaviour and other psychopathology and

· therapist factors, such as extent of clinical experience.

For whom is the treatment component of TAPP-C appropriate?

TAPP-C has been developed as a targeted therapy to be used for both the caregivers of children and adolescents between the ages of two and 17 who have been involved in firesetting or other types of fire involvement and the children themselves.

For the purposes of this manual, *fire involvement* is defined as any unsanctioned or dangerous fire-related behaviour that has been threatened, planned or carried out. Fire involvement may include, but is not limited to:

· unsanctioned igniting of matches, lighters or other ignition sources and/or accelerants ("match and/or lighter play")

· unsanctioned and/or exploratory igniting of paper, garbage, leaves or small objects ("fire play")

· intentional igniting of objects, buildings, vehicles or persons ("firesetting" or "arson" where legal charges have been laid) and

· bomb-making.

Fire involvement may occur on one occasion only or frequently. It may be carried out by individuals or by a group of individuals. It may result from impulsivity, boredom, curiosity, attention-seeking, maliciousness or a pathological interest in fire.

The children and adolescents who are appropriate for TAPP-C may be living in family homes, foster homes, group homes or residential or custodial facilities. In each context, the appropriate participants include the child or adolescent, the primary caregiver of the child or adolescent, and any caregivers with whom the child or adolescent visits regularly; for example, a non-custodial parent. On some occasions, it may be appropriate to include other family members, but that is a clinical decision best made on a case-by-case basis.

This manual is likely to be most helpful for families with children between the ages of six and 12 years and the clinicians working with them. Although TAPP-C has been used with children from two- to 17-years-old, this manual focuses on describing most fully the interventions used with the typical firesetter; that is, a child between six and 12 years of age. For children who are younger or older, it will be necessary to modify the interventions somewhat. Some appropriate modifications have been described in the Special Issues section, p. 203.

The ideal and alternative formats of the TAPP-C treatment model

The model of TAPP-C service delivery that has been used throughout the follow-up evaluation study involves two clinicians working together concurrently to help the family. One clinician works primarily with the child, and the other works primarily with the caregiver (or parent).

As described in this manual, each session begins with a joint meeting of the two clinicians and both the child and the caregiver. During the joint meeting, home practice exercises are reviewed and any obstacles to progress are identified and addressed. Following this, the parent and child are seen separately by one clinician each in order to cover the content material and skill development exercises. Each session ends with another brief joint meeting in which the caregiver and the child share with each other what they have learned, and discuss the home practice exercises for the coming week.

Currently, this is the ideal format, yet it is recognized that some agencies may not be able to provide service in this way; for instance, it may be that there are resources for only one clinician per family. Accordingly, this manual has also been designed to permit joint sessions with the caregiver and the child, with one clinician. Or a single clinician may see the caregiver and the child separately on alternating weeks, or may work through all of the caregiver sessions, then all of the child sessions. We don't recommend that there be only sessions with the caregiver or only sessions with the child as the efficacy of these alternative models of TAPP-C service delivery have not yet been evaluated.

A group format may be possible for the caregiver sessions. At this point, however, group administration of the child or adolescent component of the therapy is not generally recommended. Some evidence in the literature on antisocial behaviour suggests that providing mental health services to antisocial youth in groups may yield no treatment effects whatsoever or even exacerbate youth symptomatology (Dishion, McCord & Poulin, 1999). Other evidence, however, indicates treatment models using a multi-faceted approach, where groups for pre-adolescent children are one component, can be successful (Hrynkiw-Augimeri, Pepler & Goldberg, 1993; Bloomquist & Schnell, 2002; Earlscourt Child and Family Centre, 2001a, 2001b).

Until further research determines under what circumstances group intervention with antisocial children and youth is successful, the prudent course of action is to treat children and adolescents individually, especially in the case of adolescents.

What training is necessary to use this manual?

This is a manual for mental health clinicians who treat children and adolescents who have behaviour problems, and their families.

The clinician who intends to use this manual should be familiar with the following fields:

· normative child development

· child psychopathology

· the theory and practice of parent management training (PMT) (Cunningham, Bremner & Boyle, 1995; Kazdin, Siegel & Bass, 1992; Webster-Stratton, Hollinsworth & Kolpacoff, 1989)

· child and adolescent cognitive behaviour therapy (CBT) (Augimeri, Koegl & Goldberg, 2001; Kazdin, Bass, Siegel & Thomas, 1989; Kendall & Braswell, 1993; Larson & Lochman, 2002; Webster, Augimeri & Koegl, 2002) and

· collaborative intervention approaches (Webster-Stratton & Hancock, 1998).

In addition to this more general experience in treating child behaviour problems and the issues surrounding it, clinicians should also be familiar with:

· the assessment and treatment of fire involvement by children and adolescents and

· the empirical literature on childhood firesetting (e.g., Gaynor, 1991; Kolko, 1996; Kolko, 2001).

Ideally, the treatment component of TAPP-C should be offered as part of the full TAPP-C program, which, in addition to the TAPP-C treatment component, includes a comprehensive risk assessment of the child and his or her family by mental health professionals, and a home fire-safety check and fire-safety education provided by fire service professionals. In addition to resources that are available in the literature, TAPP-C offers specialized training for mental health professionals in assessing and treating firesetting by children and adolescents. For more information about training opportunities, contact manual authors.

As well, the TAPP-C treatment component should be viewed as part of a continuum of mental health services that may benefit children and adolescents with disruptive behaviour problems and their families.

Additional care or treatment that may be offered to the children, adolescents and families involved with TAPP-C include the following:

· outpatient, day or residential mental health treatment for the child

· family therapy

· additional PMT

· additional child CBT and/or psychotherapy and/or

· medication.

How is this manual organized?

This manual is organized into four major parts:

· Part 1 explains the program.

· Part 2 includes caregiver modules.

· Part 3 includes child modules.

· Part 4 includes information about special issues that may affect the administration of the TAPP-C treatment component, such as dealing with adolescents or dealing with children living in group home and residential facilities.

Each caregiver and child module includes:

· background information for the clinician

· psychoeducational content about the session theme to convey to the client

· in-session practice exercises to do with the client to enhance skill learning

· home practice exercises for the client to enhance generalization and

· suggestions and opportunities to assist families to work collaboratively through joint review of session content and home practices exercises with children or adolescents and caregivers together.

Worksheets are provided for photocopying at the end of each session. Child worksheets can be put together and made into a Practice Book for the child, if desired.

Part 2

TAPP-C

Fire Safety Begins at Home: Defining and Rewarding Fire-Safe Behaviours

Session at a glance

Background

The majority of children begin their firesetting or inappropriate fire involvement in the home. In addition, many children find the ignition sources for their fire involvement in the home, even when the firesetting occurs outside of the home. More importantly, almost all fatal fires involving children occur in the home. With these findings in mind, the first TAPP-C treatment session focuses on fire safety in the home.

Given the risk of injury associated with fire involvement by a child, one useful way to conceptualize inappropriate fire involvement by a child or teenager is to view fire involvement as the absence of fire-safe behaviours. All children need to learn fire-safe behaviours. They do so by growing up in environments that reinforce the acquisition and use of fire-safe behaviours.

Caregivers and other family members are children's most important teachers. The actions and words of caregivers shape children's attitudes and behaviours. It is important for caregivers to model and help their children learn fire-safe behaviours.

All children need to learn that using fire-starting materials can be dangerous because they have the potential to cause burns, serious injury and sometimes death. Young children need to learn that they are not permitted to touch any fire-starting materials. Older children and teens need to learn that they are not permitted to touch fire-starting materials without permission or supervision. Although most children eventually have formal lessons about fire safety at school, what caregivers do in the home is the first and most important education children receive about fire safety.

In this session, caregivers will learn about their role in helping their children learn fire-safe behaviours. First, caregivers will learn about the importance of having clear rules for all family members about the use of ignition materials. Caregivers will also learn about their central role in controlling access to ignition materials in the home. Towards this end, caregivers will start making a plan (1) to search the home and rid it of unnecessary ignition materials and (2) to decide where to keep any necessary ignition materials so that they are not accessible to children.

Also emphasized is the importance of encouraging the child to assume some responsibility for fire safety in the home and the importance of rewarding the child for doing so.

As well, the child's session focuses on the importance of family fire safety and efforts the child can make to help. Getting the child on board to support the caregiver's efforts to establish control over ignition materials in the home is a critical first step. Like the caregiver, the child will devise a plan to help search the home for ignition materials and will generate a list of potential rewards for doing so.

Clinicians are encouraged to review the Special Issues section, p. 203, before beginning Session 1.

Goals

· Describe the main goals of the TAPP-C program and its treatment component to the caregiver and child.

· Discuss fire involvement by children as an absence of fire-safe behaviours and stress that safety behaviours are learned.

· Define the child's inappropriate use of ignition materials as fire-dangerous behaviour.

· Define the caregiver's lack of control over access to ignition materials as fire-dangerous behaviour.

· Develop rules about the use of ignition materials in the home.

· Develop rules about the storage of ignition materials in the home.

· Discuss a plan to search for and get rid of all unnecessary fire-starting materials in the home.

· Assist the caregiver to involve the child in fire-safe behaviours.

· Help the caregiver understand the importance of rewarding fire-safe behaviours.

· Wrap up and discuss the home practice activity with the caregiver and the child.

If short of time

Your main goals are to begin establishing a therapeutic alliance and engaging the caregiver in developing a plan regarding the safe use and storage of ignition sources and accelerants in the home.

Materials needed

· paper

· pencils

· Session 1 worksheets (p. 21)

· Session 1 progress note (p. 23)

Joint meeting with caregiver and child

Guidelines: 15 minutes

Describe the intervention program.

Why is the family attending the TAPP-C program?

Ensure that the family understands that they are here because of the child's involvement with matches, lighters and other ignition materials. Emphasize that this is very *dangerous* behaviour that puts the child and others at risk for burn injury. Emphasize that TAPP-C is a family fire-safety and injury prevention program.

Clinicians need to be aware of the reporting requirements specific to their professional organization and jurisdiction. For further information on fire-specific reporting issues, please refer to the Special Issues section on Child Welfare, p. 209.

Clinician Note

At the beginning of each session, the limits of confidentiality should be reviewed, and the child and caregiver should be asked whether there have been any other episodes of fire involvement since the previous session.

This may seem counterintuitive, as the child may be less likely to self-report further fire involvement with the knowledge that the clinician can't "keep this a secret" and must deal with the issue.

However, clear, honest and consistent communication about the clinician's role and responsibilities may ultimately save the therapeutic relationship by preventing misunderstandings down the road about what the clinician can and cannot do.

What is the goal?

Explain to the caregiver and the child that the overall goal of the treatment program is to work together to make sure that the child and family stay safe from fire. How do we do this? As a team, the caregiver, child and clinician will work together to ensure that the family identifies and establishes fire-safe behaviours and that the child stops the fire involvement.

Throughout the intervention sessions, the clinician may find it helpful to reframe the child's fire involvement from an issue of "psychopathology" to one of "safety."

How do we reach the goal?

Explain to the caregiver and child what the intervention process will look like. Include the following points in your discussion:

· There will be approximately five sessions.

· Each session will last about 90 minutes.

· There are a number of activities during each session in which the caregiver and child will participate, for example, problem-solving with the clinician, role-playing, in-session learning of new skills, and reviewing home practice activities.

· By working as a team with each other and the clinicians, the caregiver and the child are going to learn and practise new skills that will help prevent further fire involvement.

· The caregiver and child each have responsibilities in working towards the successful outcome of the therapy. The caregiver and the child will both be expected to meet with the clinician each week over the next five weeks. Both of them will have home practice activities to complete each week and to report on at the next session.

· The caregiver and child will work out a reward program for the child's fire-safe behaviours. Efforts and co-operation within the session and at home will be rewarded, as agreed upon by the caregiver and child. Rewards may include social incentives such as praise and time with the caregiver, as well as tangible items, such as stickers, food and small prizes.

Clinician Note

Although it is important to establish a safe environment in which children can share information with adults, it will also be important to convey to the children that everyone (caregivers, children, clinicians) is working as a team and that information about fire involvement cannot be kept from the team. For instance, because fire involvement is a dangerous behaviour, any information about a fire-related incident told to the clinician will need to be discussed with the caregiver and any other members of the treatment team.

As part of making the covert behaviour overt, the child should not be punished for disclosing information about fire-related incidents that were *previously unknown*. The clinician should work with the caregiver to help them understand the importance of this agreement.

Nevertheless, the child needs to be aware that he or she and the caregiver will be working with the clinician to establish a plan—including consequences—to deal with any fire involvement from the present time onward. After the plan and appropriate consequences have been agreed upon, the child will know exactly what consequences to expect should he or she become involved in subsequent fire-related activity.

Caregiver alone

Help the caregiver develop a solid understanding of the importance of stopping his or her child's fire involvement.

Guidelines: 60 minutes

The most important reason to stop the child's fire involvement is that fire involvement poses a substantial risk of injury to the child, his or her family and sometimes the community. Injury is the major killer of children. Indeed, injuries kill more children than every other cause of death added together.

Fire is one of the leading causes of injury-related deaths in children. Many children who are injured or die in fires start the fires themselves. Young children are particularly vulnerable to being burned if a fire starts. They lack knowledge about the dangers and unpredictability of fire, as well as knowledge about what to do if there is a fire. They also tend to experiment with fire in places that are more difficult to escape from safely, including the following:

· inside the home as opposed to outside and

· in locations where they are hidden or enclosed, such as in a closet or under the bed.

For further information about issues related to preschoolers, please see the Special Issues section on Preschoolers, p. 206.

A second reason to intervene is the high rate of repeat fire involvement by children. Statistics indicate that without intervention, 50 per cent—or one of every two children who become involved with fire—may set another fire or be involved in another fire incident.

The high rate of repeat fire involvement, coupled with the risk of injury, are sufficient reasons to take action with any child involved with fire. In addition, TAPP-C focuses on basic fire-safety skills for caregivers and children, and these skills are of benefit for every family.

Additional reasons to address fire involvement include other potential consequences, for example, legal and financial consequences, to the child or family resulting from continued fire involvement.

Use the following questions to begin a discussion with the caregiver about TAPP-C as a family fire-safety and injury prevention program:

Why do you as a caregiver think it is important to address your child's involvement with fire?

What concerns do you have if your child's fire involvement continues?

What do we mean by *fire involvement?*

Many children and adolescents, especially those with more entrenched patterns of fire involvement, will have experimented with a variety of ignition sources.

Some children are very creative in their fire involvement and have used ignition sources that may not immediately come to mind for the caregiver. As the caregiver is learning strategies for dealing with the child's fire involvement, he or she should be thinking about fire involvement as including the unsanctioned use of any ignition material.

> *If available, review the child's history of fire involvement and use of fire-starting materials other than matches or lighters. Use some of the following questions to help the caregiver define fire-dangerous behaviour as the inappropriate use of any potential ignition source.*

- **What types of fire-related behaviour has your child engaged in?**

- **What ignition sources has your child used?**

- **Has your child used matches or lighters?**

- **What about things like the stove, the microwave oven, the toaster, candles, the barbeque or the fireplace? Has your child ever used these ignition sources in inappropriate ways?**

- **Has there been any inappropriate use of (other non-conventional) ignition sources, such as the pilot light on the stove or a blowtorch?**

- **Has your child used accelerants (e.g., gasoline, lighter fluid)? What type?**

What framework is best for helping children stop inappropriate fire involvement?

The TAPP-C framework is based on the following premises:

1. Juvenile fire involvement indicates an absence of fire-safe behaviours.

2. Fire-related behaviours are learned.

3. The family home (or alternative caregiver setting) is an important setting for learning fire-safe behaviours.

Any unsanctioned use of matches, lighters or other ignition materials by a child should be considered fire-dangerous behaviour. It indicates that the child has not learned, or does not practise, fire-safe behaviours. Fire-safety knowledge and attitudes may also be lacking.

TAPP-C is a program that will help modify fire-related behaviours. The family and the child will learn and practise new fire-related behaviours.

The goals of intervention are to develop fire-safe behaviours; for example, establishing clear rules about who may and may not use matches and lighters or other ignition sources, and to eliminate fire-dangerous behaviours; for example, leaving matches and lighters where children are able to access them.

As fire-safe behaviours are learned and practised by the family, and knowledge about fire safety is acquired, beliefs about the importance of fire safety may also emerge.

Use some of the following questions to orient the caregiver to the TAPP-C framework for understanding or conceptualizing juvenile fire involvement:

- **What do you think your child needs to learn to stop the fire involvement?**

- **What can you, the caregiver, do to help stop the fire involvement?**

Help the caregiver understand that most safety behaviours are learned.

Use questions about the family's use of car seat belts (or some other safety behaviour like not taking medicine without permission) to help the caregiver understand that children must learn how to keep themselves safe and that the caregiver and other family members are important teachers, especially in terms of the behaviours they demonstrate or model for their children.

- **Does your child wear a seat belt when riding in a car? How did your child learn this safety rule?**

- **Do you or someone else your child observes wear a seat belt?**

- **What message do you think putting on a seat belt sends to your child?**

- **What message would it send to your child if you did not use a seat belt or if you did not make your child use a seat belt?**

Help the caregiver make rules about the use of matches and lighters or other ignition sources that everyone in the home must follow.

Most families have implicit rules about the use of ignition sources. These types of rules should be considered the backbone of family fire safety, but *the rules need to be stated clearly and explicitly.* There should be rules for the children, adolescents and adults. For example:

· For safety reasons, young children should *never* be allowed to touch matches and lighters.

This rule is clear and easy to understand even for very young children. The rule should be stated explicitly. Other caretakers of the children, such as grandparents or babysitters, should be told of this rule. *No one should allow the child to break this rule.*

· Older children should only be allowed to touch ignition sources with permission and/or supervision as negotiated with the caregivers.

The conditions under which older children are permitted to use ignition sources also need to be stated explicitly.

· Adults should only use matches, lighters or other ignition sources as tools to perform certain tasks, such as lighting cigarettes or candles. Adults should never use ignition sources in playful, dangerous or reckless ways.

Some people use fire in their household responsibilities or as part of their religious, cultural or spiritual practices. Please see the relevant Special Issues sections, p. 204, for more information.

> *Use some of the following questions to help the caregiver think about his or her family's rules regarding ignition sources and to complete the* Family Safety Rules for Ignition Materials *worksheet.*

- **Does your family have rules about the use of ignition sources? For example, are there any explicit rules about the use of matches or lighters in your home?**

- **Are the rules different for adults versus children? Why or why not?**

- **Should your child be permitted to use matches or lighters? Why or why not?**

- **What message do such rules convey to your child?**

- **What message does the absence of such rules convey to your child?**

Help the caregiver get on board with the importance of caregiver control over access to ignition sources in the home.

As already noted, the majority of children begin their firesetting behaviour or fire involvement in the home.

Also, many children use matches or lighters found in the home as the ignition sources for their fire involvement, even when the firesetting occurs outside of the home.

The link between access to ignition materials and fire involvement is unequivocal: one cannot start a fire without ignition materials.

Use some of the following questions to engage the caretaker in a discussion about the link between access to ignition materials and fire involvement by the child and hence the importance of establishing caregiver control over access to ignition materials in the home.

- What types of fire-starting materials has your child used in the past?

- Where can your child get these materials?

- Where do most children obtain their fire-starting materials?

- Do you think there is a connection between being able to get ignition sources and your child using them?

- Does your child know where in your home there are matches and lighters?

- Where does your family keep matches and lighters?

- How does this compare with where your family keeps other hazardous items, such as medication or guns?

- What message does how hazardous items are stored convey to your child?

- Are there safer or more secure places that matches and lighters could be stored?

- What are the advantages of storing fire-starting materials in a more secure way?

- What other potential fire-starting materials are in there in your home? For example, do you have a barbeque starter, blowtorch, gasoline or other accelerants in your home? Could they also be stored in more secure ways?

Help the caregiver make a plan to get rid of all unnecessary fire-starting materials.

Discuss with the caregiver the importance of home fire-safety searches.

Once the caregiver has gained some understanding of why caregiver control over ignition materials is an important fire-safe behaviour, the clinician can help the caregiver complete questions 1 and 2 of the *Home Fire-Safety Search* worksheet by developing a plan for doing the following:

· searching the home for ignition materials

· getting rid of all unnecessary materials and

· deciding where to keep necessary materials so that they are not accessible to children.

This "safety-proofing" plan for ignition materials should include a room-by-room search of the home and other properties, including garages, sheds, trailers, cars and/or cottages.

The child and the caregiver should do this together, as the child may be aware of ignition sources the caregiver has long forgotten or may have his or her own stash of which the caregiver is unaware.

Also, the searching is something the child can be good at, and encourages the child to participate and get on board with the commitment to making the home fire-safe.

Ask the following questions to promote the idea that the family is a team, and everyone in the family should be involved in making sure that ignition sources are kept and stored away from children:

- **How could your family get rid of any unnecessary ignition materials?**
- **Where do you need to search for ignition materials?**
- **When should this search occur?**

Clinician Note

When discussing home fire-safety searches, it may be necessary to review with the caregiver all of the areas of the home that need to be checked, particularly the following:

· the child's bedroom

· any play areas

· kitchen drawers and cupboards

· bookshelves

· vehicles

· garages and

· basements.

These are often storage areas for ignition sources and accelerants.

It is often helpful to discuss with the caregiver several appropriate ways and places in which to securely store fire materials.

Many caregivers believe it is sufficient to place such materials in an inconvenient but unlocked location, such as in a high cupboard. However, for most families, ignition materials need to be securely locked, and not simply stored out of sight.

Many children and adolescents have told us how they have accessed fire materials in seemingly secure—but unlocked—locations. They have described taking lighters from underneath their parent's pillow while they slept, climbing onto counters to access items kept in high cupboards, and discovering their parents' "secret" hiding places for matches and lighters without their parents' knowledge.

Caregivers can lock up ignition materials in a lock box that can be purchased at larger department or hardware stores. An alternative is to place a padlock on a drawer or cupboard door containing ignition sources and accelerants.

If there are any fire materials stored in the basement, garage or shed of a home, such as gasoline, paint, welding tools or torches, it is highly recommended that the caregiver place a lock on the door of the room or building containing these materials.

In the case of caregivers who smoke, it is important to have them generate ideas for the storage of their lighter while they are asleep and together with the clinician determine the best storage solution.

Help the caregiver get the child actively involved in carrying out the fire-safety plan for the home.

It is important for the caregiver to provide the child with opportunities to assume some responsibility for his or her own safety.

Enlisting the child's help in carrying out the search for ignition materials is one such opportunity. This also begins the process of replacing negative behaviours (fire-dangerous behaviours) with positive ones (fire-safe behaviours).

Ask the following questions to promote the idea that all children, even very young ones, can be good at some aspect of fire safety and should be provided with opportunities, encouragement and lots of praise for fire-safe behaviours:

- **How could your child help with the search of the home?**

- **Why is it important to get your child on board with home fire-safety activities?**

- **How can you enlist your child's help or co-operation?**

- **What message do you want to send your child about his or her role regarding fire safety?**

- **Could your child be involved in educating other members of your family about the importance of the home search?**

Help the caregiver complete question 3 of the *Home Fire-Safety Search* worksheet.

Use the following questions to engage the caregiver in understanding the value of providing rewards for the child's efforts at fire safety. Help the caregiver complete question 4 of the Home Fire-Safety Search *worksheet.*

- **Why is it important to reward your child's efforts at using positive or safe behaviours?**

- **What message does the reward send your child?**

- **What are the different kinds of rewards (tangible vs. social, praise, hugs, etc.)?**

- **What kinds of rewards does your child like?**

- **What kinds of rewards are you able to offer?**

Clinician Note

The reward to the child is for effort at helping the caregiver carry out the search of the home and not for bringing fire-starting materials to the caregiver.

Children should never be encouraged or rewarded for picking up or touching fire-starting materials.

The home search should only be conducted when a caregiver is present. If the child comes across ignition sources at other times, he or she should be instructed not to touch them but to leave them and to tell an adult where they are located.

Wrap-up and joint meeting with caregiver and child

Guidelines: 15 minutes

Provide a brief review of the content of the session and an overview of the family's home practice exercise.

This week the family's home practice exercise is to conduct a search of the home and reward themselves for doing so.

Discuss with the caregiver and child how they can use the *Home Fire-Safety Search* worksheet to guide their practice. Review the child's *Home Map* worksheet, p. 116, and problem-solve solutions to any of the anticipated difficulties noted by the caregiver or child in completing the home practice activities. Focus on the efforts at co-operation between the caregiver and child and provide liberal praise and recognition for these efforts.

Have the child practise telling other family members who were not present at the session about what he or she learned and about the goal of searching the home for fire safety.

Have the caregiver and child discuss potential times they could do the search of the home and have them plan or practise how they would search a room together.

Use the child's *Stickers and Rewards: What I Can Earn at Home* worksheet, p. 117, to discuss the prize, stickers or social incentives that the family will be able to earn if the home practice activities are completed.

Discuss home practice.

The following are the suggested home practice activities to be completed before the next session:

1. The caregiver and child should talk to other family members about the importance of family fire-safety practices and the purpose of the home fire-safety search.

2. The caregiver should post the *Home Fire-Safety Search* worksheet in a prominent place at home and use it to track the fire-safety search activities.

Clinician Note

The clinician should keep a copy of this *Home Fire-Safety Search* worksheet in the family's file for subsequent sessions.

3. The caregiver and child should complete a search of the home, and the caregiver should destroy all unnecessary ignition materials and/or accelerants and lock up those that are kept.

4. With the help of his or her caregiver, the child should complete the *Home Practice Checklist*, page 118, to check off the tasks completed.

5. The family members should reward themselves for searching the home for ignition materials and for finding an appropriate place to lock up necessary ignition materials and/or accelerants.

Family Safety Rules for Ignition Materials

1. These family members are *not* permitted to:

   e.g., Johnny is not allowed to touch lighters or other ignition materials.

   These family members are permitted to:

   e.g., Dad is allowed to keep one lighter.

2. The family has agreed to store ignition materials in the following places:

   e.g., Dad will keep his lighter in his pocket or locked up.

TAPP-C
Worksheet

Caregiver

Home Fire-Safety Search

1. Where to check for ignition materials and/or accelerants:

   e.g., Johnny's bedroom and playroom, kitchen and living room, garage and car

2. When to check:

   e.g., After supper on Tuesdays and Fridays

3. Who will check:

   e.g., Mom, Dad and Johnny together

4. Reward for checking:

   e.g., Rent video chosen by Johnny

TAPP-C
Progress Note

• Caregiver

Fire Safety Begins at Home:
Defining and Rewarding Fire-Safe Behaviour

Name: _____   File no.: _____   Session date: _____

Action plan:

☐ Client cancelled (specify action plan)   _____

☐ No show (specify action plan)   _____

☐ Clinician cancelled (specify action plan)   _____

☐ Attended Session 1 of the TAPP-C program

Fire involvement since last session?   ☐ Yes   ☐ No

Fire-safety education: ☐ In progress   ☐ Done   ☐ Not started   ☐ N/A

This session covered the following:

Covered	*Not covered*	
☐	☐	Began with joint meeting with caregiver and child
☐	☐	Reviewed goals and importance of the TAPP-C program
☐	☐	Defined fire involvement as the inappropriate use of any ignition sources
☐	☐	Discussed fire involvement as an absence of fire-safe behaviours by the child and family
☐	☐	Discussed that safety behaviours are learned
☐	☐	Developed rules about use of ignition materials in the home
☐	☐	Developed rules about where to keep ignition materials in the home
☐	☐	Discussed plan to get rid of all unnecessary fire-starting materials
☐	☐	Discussed involving child in carrying out the search of the home
☐	☐	Developed a plan to reward effort at completing the search
☐	☐	Ended with joint meeting with caregiver and child
☐	☐	Discussed home practice

Outcome of session:

☐ Next session scheduled for: _____

☐ Treatment terminated (client initiated)   ☐ Treatment terminated (clinician initiated)

Additional notes:

_____   _____
Signature/Credentials   Date

Fire Safety Continues at Home: Monitoring Access to Ignition Materials and Learning SNAP™

Session at a glance

Background

It is important in this session to re-emphasize to the caregiver and child the connection between access to fire-related materials and the child's fire involvement. Participants should view control of access to ignition materials as fundamental to home fire safety.

Toward this end, a process will need to be developed for monitoring that all family members and visitors to the home are following the explicitly stated rules regarding the following:

· where to keep matches and lighters and

· where to keep other ignition sources.

The monitoring of ignition materials should become a regular family routine.

Everyone needs to understand that this is a routine to keep the family and the child safe from fire. This type of routine is also a powerful message to the child about the family's views about the importance of fire safety.

Families participating in the TAPP-C intervention have been quite successful in stopping their child's fire involvement. Nevertheless, some children who stopped their fire involvement, even for extended periods of time, did become reinvolved with fire. Our follow-up data suggest that for some of these children, the family stopped using the TAPP-C fire-safety practices, such as monitoring the home for ignition materials, because they believed that the child had lost interest in fire.

Remind participants that some of the new fire-safe behaviours they are using to control access to ignition materials are replacing their old fire-dangerous behaviours. Most of these behaviours or routines should continue indefinitely.

Ideally, if more intrusive measures to keep ignition materials secure are required, like ones that may involve searching the child's belongings on return from the community, these can be stopped as the child becomes free from fire involvement over a prolonged time interval.

Goals

· Check in with the caregiver and child.

· Review the home practice with the caregiver and child.

· Plan steps to ensure that new ignition materials and/or accelerants do not come into the home.

· Develop rules for adolescents or others in the home who smoke.

· Plan ways to monitor compliance with rules regarding ignition materials in the home.

· Discuss how to involve the child in carrying out the monitoring of home fire-safety practices and possible rewards for doing so.

· Wrap up and discuss the home practice activities with the caregiver and child.

If short of time

Your main goals are to problem-solve strategies with the caregiver for:

· keeping new ignition materials out of the home and

· monitoring compliance with rules about ignition materials in the home.

Materials needed

· paper

· pencils

· Session 2 worksheets (p. 37)

· Session 2 progress note (p. 39)

Joint meeting of caregiver and child

Guidelines: 15 minutes

Check-in

Have there been any further episodes of fire involvement since the last appointment?

If no further fire involvement is reported by the caregiver or child, assume the best and praise both participants for their efforts and good work.

If further fire involvement has occurred, model for the caregiver and child an appropriate response that includes recognizing the seriousness of this behaviour and the need for problem-solving to determine what went wrong, as well as how to intervene further. (See Clinician Note.)

Clinician Note

An incident of fire-related relapse provides a good opportunity for the clinician to model an appropriate response that includes problem-solving what went wrong, establishing appropriate and meaningful consequences, and further tailoring the intervention to meet the family's needs.

Obtain specific details from the child as to the circumstances surrounding the fire-related incident. For instance, the child could be asked the following questions:

What ignition source was used? Where was the ignition source obtained? Where did the incident take place? Was anyone else involved? What was the child thinking and feeling just prior to the incident? How long has the child been thinking of doing this? What could have prevented it (from the child's point of view)?

· Introduce to the caregiver the notion of separating "education" from "consequences." While it is important that the child recognize the seriousness of his or her behaviour, now is probably not the best time for the clinician or caregiver to get into a lengthy review about the dangers of fire. The clinician can note that children and teens are likely to feel strong emotions during this time, such as anger at being caught or anxiety about how this will be dealt with. Therefore, highlight to caregivers that this is not an optimal time for learning. For instance, the clinician can let the child know that his or her actions were dangerous, but that further discussion of the incident will be saved for tomorrow. (As part of their home practice, ask the caregiver and child to further process the incident at home the following day. For instance, how much has the child retained from the first two sessions? Can he or she discuss how this particular incident was dangerous? What were the potential consequences?)

· Remind the participants that developing a proactive plan and appropriate consequences for dealing with any further fire involvement is part of the TAPP-C program and will be covered in detail in Session 4.

· Nevertheless, given that the child has been reinvolved with fire, now is an opportune time to have a preliminary discussion about consequences.

· What consequences could be given? (e.g., What privilege could be withdrawn, and for how long?) Ask the caregiver to anticipate any problem that may arise with the consequence given, and problem-solve potential strategies for dealing with the obstacle(s). If the clinician has time, he or she can offer to call at a designated time during the week to ensure that the consequences are followed through as planned. At the very least, make it clear that the consequences will be discussed during the following session.

· Importantly, the information obtained about this fire-related incident will help the clinician to target further intervention (which can be built into today's session and/or home practice). For instance, if the child obtained a lighter from the kitchen cupboard, further problem-solving should explore how to prevent access to ignition materials within the home.

If appropriate, ask the following question:

What is your family's status and progress with the Fire Service Education portion of TAPP-C?

Review of home practice

Review the home practice from Session 1 (p. 20) with the caregiver and child. Ask the following questions:

Did you or your child talk to other family members about the first TAPP-C session and about the home fire-safety search?

How did the other family members react?

Did the family carry out the initial home fire-safety search activities?

Did the family decide on a secure location in which to keep ignition materials?

Did you reward carrying out the search?

Did the family post the *Home Fire-Safety Search* worksheet, p. 22, in a prominent place and use it to record fire-safe behaviours?

When the family was able to carry out the home practice, ask the following question:

What did the caregiver and child find helpful about these new home fire-safety activities?

Have them talk about these behaviours so that they may become more aware of their usefulness. Be generous with your compliments for a job well done. Everyone enjoys recognition for their efforts. You are trying to encourage all family members to value fire safety. Model the powerful effect of positive reinforcement for the caregiver.

When the family was unable or unwilling to carry out the home practice, ask the following questions:

What prevented you from carrying out the home practice activities?

Can you think of ways to overcome these obstacles?

The clinician should use a collaborative, problem-solving approach to work with the family on how to accomplish the goal of searching the home for fire materials in the coming week. Help them to generate a feasible plan, noting that other families have also had difficulties in implementing these changes, and that there are solutions to these barriers. Review the *Home Fire-Safety Search* worksheet with the caregiver and child and get them to agree to try the home practice in the coming week.

Remind participants that keeping matches, lighters and other ignition sources away from the child is the single most important and probably the easiest step that they can take to stop the child's fire involvement.

Clinician Note

The agenda for Session 2 should not begin until you are satisfied that the family understands the importance of controlling access to ignition materials as a basic rule of fire safety, as well as the importance of rewarding the child's fire-safe behaviours when they occur.

Keep in mind that it is optimal to add intervention sessions until both the caregiver and child have had an opportunity to experience at least partial success in each of their home practice activities. If extra sessions will be necessary, explore this option with the caregiver and child.

Review the Special Issues section on The Reluctant or Resistant Caregiver, p. 203.

Caregiver alone

Guidelines: 60 minutes

Help the family make sure that new matches, lighters or other ignition sources do not come into the home.

The goal is to help the caregiver plan a list of additional rules and/or steps that he or she may need to take to keep matches, lighters or other ignition sources under caregiver control, that is, from being available in the home unknowingly.

Families where members smoke present unique challenges for controlling access to ignition materials. In our experience, it is not unusual for smokers to have many lighters in multiple locations within the home, the car and so on. As such, caregivers who have smokers in the home will need to use extra caution in making sure that matches and lighters are kept secure and out of the hands of children.

One very simple way to control the whereabouts of smoking materials is to have a rule that each smoker is permitted to have only one lighter.

Lighters are preferred over matches because lighters are easier to keep track of, particularly since it is difficult to notice when one or two matches are missing from a pack. Smokers must then keep their lighter on them at all times or locked up when they are sleeping. If their lighter does go missing for whatever reason, the smoker will quickly become aware of its absence and can take appropriate steps to find it. When there are multiple lighters on the premises, it is more difficult to notice when one has gone missing or is available to children.

Some TAPP-C sites have given caregivers inexpensive waist pouches for the safekeeping of smoking materials.

Visitors to the home may need to be apprised that the family takes great care with fire safety and does not permit anyone to leave a lighter unattended or not on their person.

If the child is likely to bring or has brought matches and lighters into the home in the past, then a plan needs to include rules about searching the child's pockets and belongings when the child returns home from the community. These search rules need to be:

· negotiated with the child

· stated explicitly

· never used as punishment and

· never conducted covertly, but with the knowledge and co-operation of the child.

Searches of the child, or the child's room and belongings (which also should never be done covertly), should be framed as strategies to help keep the child and the family safe.

Clinician Note

With regard to searches of the child, several issues need to be considered. Searching is not intended to be a punishment; it is a measure that is being taken to improve fire safety in the home. Accordingly, it is important to consider how the process can be made most comfortable for the child.

First, consider how the child is likely to react to searches. For instance, some children feel embarrassed and do best when taken aside and searched privately (away from siblings and/or peers). Others may feel angry about personal searches and view them as an invasion of their privacy.

Second, consider what the scope of the search should be. For instance, some children have been known to hide their ignition sources in the garage, shed or yard.

Caregivers may benefit from a discussion or role-play that includes how best to deal with their child's reaction, as well as how to make their search as comprehensive as is needed.

Ask the following questions to help participants complete the Additional Rules for Keeping Ignition Materials and Accelerants under Caregiver Control *worksheet.*

- **Do any of your family members or visitors smoke?**

- **How can people who smoke in your house keep track of their lighters or matches? What extra measures can you ask them to take?**

- **How else do matches and lighters come into your home?**

- **What needs to be done to prevent new matches and lighters from coming into your home?**

- **Has your child ever brought matches or lighters into your home?**

- **What extra steps need to be taken to ensure that your child does not bring new ignition materials into your home?**

What can be done to reduce access to ignition materials for a youth who smokes?

The child or adolescent smoker with a history of fire involvement presents unique challenges. These youth should be prohibited from carrying matches or lighters. Note that the Court almost always imposes this type of restriction for any youth convicted of a fire-related offence. Indeed, court-ordered sanctions for firesetting sometimes include prohibitions against the possession of any incendiary device, including a lit cigarette.

For more information, please see the section on Adolescents in Special Issues, p. 207.

If the caregiver or youth is contemplating or is motivated to stop smoking, you should reinforce this idea and begin to problem-solve the steps toward achieving this goal. Part of this includes providing information; for example, on smoking cessation programs in the local community. Discuss the level of involvement that the youth or caregiver could expect from you, even if you are only "checking in" on her or his progress.

Unfortunately, it has been our experience that older youth or caregivers are rarely willing to consider giving up smoking. If the youth is going to continue to smoke, then a plan should be negotiated with the caregiver and youth about where he or she is permitted to smoke and about how he or she is going to obtain a light for cigarettes.

Many adolescents who set a fire or use fire inappropriately do not do so in a malicious or planned way. Rather, many of these youth tend to be impulsive and have a history of playing with their lighters in a more habitual or mindless way. They use their lighter or matches without thinking—because they have immediate access to these ignition sources in their pockets or purses.

A very effective way to prevent the impulsive use of a lighter by an adolescent is to restrict him or her from carrying a lighter or matches. When the adolescent does want to smoke, he or she will have to seek out a lighter (and possibly adult supervision). The delay that becomes necessary to accomplish this will, in and of itself, help prevent impulsive or unplanned fire involvement.

Many adolescents are aware, or can be made aware, of the impulsive or habitual nature of their lighter play. They often agree to not carry lighters or matches as a way of preventing impulsive use of fire when the strategy and its rationale are explained to them and concerns about their safety or criminal liability are highlighted.

Use the following questions to help the caregiver think about rules for the adolescent and possibly for other family members or visitors who smoke.

- **Does your teenager smoke?**
- **Are there rules about your teenager's smoking? For example, where and when is your teenager permitted to smoke?**
- **Should there be rules about your teenager's smoking?**
- **Why would such rules be helpful?**
- **Should there be rules about your teenager's access to smoking materials?**
- **What would the goals of these rules be?**
- **What about other smokers in your home? Should there be rules for these individuals?**
- **What message might such rules convey to your teenager?**

Help the family monitor that everyone is following the rules about where to keep matches or lighters in the home.

Use the following questions to guide the caregiver to think about monitoring access to ignition materials as an ongoing fire-safety behaviour. Have the caregiver use his or her answers to update the family's previously completed Home Fire-Safety Search *worksheet, p. 22.*

How can your family check to make sure that everyone is following the family's rules about where to keep matches, lighters and other ignition sources?

Would it be helpful to regularly check the home to make sure that matches or lighters are not left unattended or in places that are accessible to your child?

How often do you think this checking should occur?

How could your child be of help in conducting these checks?

What message would this send to your child?

How could your family remember to do these checks?

Help the family decide how to reward the regular home fire-safety checks.

Use the following questions to remind the caregiver about the importance of reinforcing positive behaviours. Have the caregiver use the answers to update question 4 of the Home Fire-Safety Search *worksheet that deals with rewards.*

How did your child respond to being rewarded for helping with your home search?

How should your child (or entire family) be rewarded for regularly checking that everyone is following the rules about keeping and storing matches and lighters in a safe fashion?

When should a reward be given?

Clinician Note

The reward provided is for the child's effort at helping the caregiver with the searching and/or monitoring of ignition materials. It is not good practice to make the reward contingent on not finding matches or lighters. This may only encourage the child to become more lax with the searches or more devious about hiding fire-starting materials.

Session 4 will focus on effective consequences and how the caregiver should respond if the child is found with matches or lighters or is involved in another episode of fire involvement.

Wrap-up and joint meeting with caregiver and child

Guidelines: 15 minutes

Provide a brief review of the content of the session and the updates to the *Home Fire-Safety Search* worksheet.

Focus on the co-operative efforts of the caregiver and child and provide liberal praise and recognition for these efforts.

Have the caregiver explain any additional rules (e.g., for smokers) regarding ignition materials in the home. Have the child practise telling other family members who were not present at the session about these rules with the goal of enlisting their help and co-operation. This is an excellent venue for getting the child on board with the new rules.

If the child has already had the session that introduces SNAP™, help the child teach the caregiver about Stop Now And Plan (SNAP™)[1] and demonstrate its use.

Have the caregiver and child practise a pocket and/or bag search together, if it will be required in the home.

---

[1] See Child Session 2 for details about SNAP™. This manual contains trademarked materials under license granted by Earlscourt Child and Family Centre.

Discuss home practice.

The following are the suggested home practice activities to be completed before the next session:

1. The caregiver should post the updated Home Fire-Safety Search worksheet.

2. The caregiver and child should schedule two occasions when together they will check that matches, lighters and other ignition materials are being stored as planned.

3. The caregiver should help the child practise SNAP™ in actual problematic situations that occur for the child. However, if such occasions do not occur naturally, the caregiver should schedule two times before the next session to help the child practise (e.g., role-play) SNAP™. The caregiver should also help the child complete two *SNAP™ Tracking Sheets*.

4. The caregiver should reward the family for checking to insure that ignition sources and/or accelerants in the home are secure and that new ignition sources and/or accelerants have not come into the home. The caregiver should reward the child for practising SNAP™.

5. The caregiver and child should together complete the *Home Practice Checklist*, p. 143, to record what home practice activities have been completed.

Additional Rules for Keeping Ignition Materials and Accelerants under Caregiver Control

1. e.g., Johnny will empty his pockets and school bag when coming into the house.

2. e.g., Dad will check his pockets for lighters when coming home from work.

3. e.g., Visitors to the home will be reminded to carry their lighters with them.

2 Session

TAPP-C
Progress Note

• Caregiver

Fire Safety Continues at Home: Monitoring Access to Ignition Materials and Learning SNAP™

Name: _____ File no.: _____ Session date: _____

Action plan:

☐ Client cancelled (specify action plan) _____

☐ No show (specify action plan) _____

☐ Clinician cancelled (specify action plan) _____

☐ Attended Session 2 of the TAPP-C program

Fire involvement since last session?   ☐ Yes   ☐ No

Fire-safety education: ☐ In progress   ☐ Done   ☐ Not started   ☐ N/A

This session covered the following:

Covered	*Not covered*	
☐	☐	Began with joint meeting/check-in with caregiver and child
☐	☐	Reviewed previous home practice
☐	☐	Discussed ensuring that new ignition materials do not come into the home
☐	☐	Developed rules for searching the youth on entry to the home
☐	☐	Developed rules for adolescents who smoke cigarettes
☐	☐	Developed rules for others who smoke in the home
☐	☐	Discussed checking/monitoring ignition materials in the home
☐	☐	Developed a plan to reward monitoring of ignition materials
☐	☐	Ended with joint meeting with caregiver and child
☐	☐	Discussed home practice
☐	☐	Helped the child teach the caregiver about SNAP™

Outcome of session:

☐ Next session scheduled for: _____

☐ Treatment terminated (client initiated)   ☐ Treatment terminated (clinician initiated)

Additional notes:

_____   _____

Signature/Credentials   Date

Session 2 • Caregiver   **39**

Copyright © 2004 • Centre for Addiction and Mental Health • Office of the Fire Marshal of Ontario

Fire Safety Away from Home: Preventing Situations that Lead to Fire Involvement

Session at a glance

Background

Sessions 1 and 2 focused on establishing rules, routines and rewards within the family home to promote fire-safe behaviour. This session emphasizes strategies for insuring fire safety when the child is away from the primary caregiver.

Specifically, this session will show how to take a proactive stance in preventing situations that may lead to fire involvement when the child is outside of his or her primary caregiver's supervision.

Highlighted in this session is the importance of sharing information with other individuals who will be supervising the child regarding the child's fire involvement and the fire-safety practices that can be used to prevent such involvement.

Common antecedents to a child's fire involvement will be identified and the caregiver will develop and practise skills for controlling and monitoring the child's whereabouts in order to prevent exposure to situations and persons that may promote fire-dangerous behaviours.

Goals

· Check in with the caregiver and child.

· Review last week's home practice with the caregiver and child.

· Discuss how to reduce risk when the child is with other caregivers.

· Discuss how to reduce risk when the child is not supervised and review common antecedents to fire involvement.

· Help the caregiver plan ahead for times when the child is unsupervised.

· Wrap up and discuss the new home practice activities with the caregiver and child.

If short of time

Your main goals are to assist the caregiver in identifying the child's key supervision needs, and to begin to develop proactive strategies for effective supervision and monitoring.

Materials needed

· paper

· pencils

· Session 3 worksheets (p. 53)

· Session 3 progress note (p. 59)

Joint meeting with caregiver and child

Guidelines: 15 minutes

Check-in

Have there been any further episodes of fire involvement since the last appointment?

If no further fire involvement is reported by the caregiver or child, assume the best and praise both participants for their efforts and good work.

If further fire involvement has occurred, model for the caregiver and child an appropriate response that includes recognizing the seriousness of the behaviour and the need for problem-solving to determine what went wrong, as well as how to intervene further. (For further details, see Clinician Note, Session 2, p. 28.)

An incident of fire-related relapse provides a good opportunity for in-session review and further learning about:

· prevention of situations that lead to fire involvement

· the importance of controlling access to ignition materials and accelerants and

· practising with SNAP™.

If appropriate, ask the following question:

What is the status and progress of your family with the Fire Service Education portion of TAPP-C?

Review of home practice

Review the home practice from Session 2 (p. 36) with the caregiver and child. Ask the following questions:

Did the caregiver and child discuss any additional rules about ignition sources and accelerants or home checks with other family members?

Did your family check your home for ignition materials?

Is your family keeping ignition sources in the agreed upon ways?

Did the child practise SNAP™?

Did your family use the *Home Fire-Safety Search* worksheet, p. 22, to record these activities?

Did you reward carrying out these fire-safety behaviours?

> *When the family was able to carry out the home practice, ask the following question:*

■ **What did the caregiver and the child find helpful about these new home fire-safety activities?**

Have them talk about these behaviours so that they may become more aware of their usefulness. Be generous with your compliments for a job well done. Everyone enjoys recognition for their efforts. You are trying to encourage all family members to value fire safety. Model the powerful effect of positive reinforcement for the caregiver.

> *When the family was unable or unwilling to carry out the home practice, ask the following questions:*

■ **What prevented you from carrying out the home practice activities?**

■ **Can you think of ways to overcome these obstacles?**

The clinician should use a collaborative, problem-solving approach to work with the family on how to accomplish the goal of completing the home practice activities. Review the *Home Fire-Safety Search* worksheet, p. 22, with the caregiver and child and get them to agree to try the home practice activities in the coming week.

Remind participants that keeping matches, lighters and other ignition sources away from the child is the single most important and probably the easiest step that they can take to stop the child's fire involvement.

Clinician Note

The agenda for Session 3 should not begin until you are satisfied that the caregiver and child understand the importance of limiting access to incendiaries, monitoring the home for access to them, limiting new ignition materials from coming into the home and rewarding fire-safe behaviours when they occur.

Keep in mind that it is optimal to add intervention sessions until the caregiver and the child have each had an opportunity to experience at least partial success in each of their home practice activities. If extra sessions are needed, explore this option with the caregiver and child.

Review the Special Issues section on The Reluctant or Resistant Caregiver, p. 203.

Caregiver alone

Guidelines: 60 minutes

Reduce risk of fire involvement when the child is being supervised by an alternate caregiver.

Many children seen for fire involvement spend time with different caretakers in different settings. Primary caregivers sometimes fail to tell other persons about their child's fire involvement for a variety of reasons.

Some caregivers are embarrassed by their child's fire involvement. Others believe that sharing information about their child's fire involvement will be hurtful to the child because it may result in the child being discriminated against, labelled and/or possibly excluded from activities that could benefit him or her.

However, many caregivers fail to tell others about the child's fire involvement because they do not realize that it is helpful to do so.

It is important for caregivers to understand that there are a number of reasons for sharing information about their child's fire involvement with others.

First, it is very likely that the child will have access to ignition sources in different locations. While the most common place that a child obtains access to ignition sources is in his or her own home, the second most common place is in the homes of others. Unfortunately, many individuals are not aware of the potential danger of ignition materials being available to children.

A second reason for informing others who will be supervising the child about the child's fire involvement is that once they are aware of the child's fire interest, they too can be of assistance in both keeping the child safe and in helping the child learn fire-safe behaviours. Like the child's primary caregiver, these individuals can model fire-safe behaviours (like keeping ignition materials away from children) and provide appropriate monitoring in situations that may lead to the access of ignition materials.

The primary caregiver should strive to get all significant others to present a united front to the child with regard to fire-safety rules and expectations.

Clinician Note

Whether or not to inform school officials of the child's fire involvement can be a tricky issue. Generally, information sharing with the school should be on a "need to know" basis in order to protect the child's right to confidentiality.

However, the child's rights need to be balanced against safety concerns. In discussing the issue with the caregiver and child, consider the following questions: What is the child's history of fire involvement? Where did the fire involvement occur? What was the apparent motive for fire involvement? What is the risk of further fire involvement?

Use some of the following questions to guide the caregiver's thinking about the importance of getting other caregivers to comply with fire-safety routines for the child:

- **Does your child spend time with other caregivers?**

- **What kind of information is important to share with other people who take care of your child?**

- **Is it possible for your child to become involved with fire while under the care of someone else?**

- **Could these individuals help keep your child fire-safe?**

- **What kinds of things could you do to help prevent your child's involvement with fire while under the care of someone else?**

- **What kind of information would help other caregivers keep your child safe?**

Use the *Information to Share with Other Caregivers* worksheet to help the caregiver plan (1) who should be informed about the child's fire interest or involvement and (2) what these people should be told.

After the worksheet has been completed, model for the caregiver how to share fire-safety information with others. Then, get the caregiver to practise (role-play) telling someone about his or her child's fire involvement and the safety steps that will help keep the child safe. Provide feedback about the caregiver's performance.

Problem-solve with the caregiver about any barriers the caregiver might anticipate in telling significant others about the child's fire involvement.

Reduce risk of fire involvement when the child is unsupervised.

When do children become involved with fire?

Most children become involved with fire when they are not being supervised. The absence of adult supervision is a common correlate of fire involvement, as well as most other antisocial behaviours. Similarly, the literature on preventing injuries links childhood injuries to a lack of appropriate supervision.

Unlike older children, who tend to be involved with fire outside of the house, young children tend to be involved with fire in the home. Yet ironically, caregivers often believe that children are safe within the home as long as there is an adult present in the home. They do not think of supervision as having "eyes or ears on the child."

It is important to consider any time when the child is not in the presence of an adult, no matter how brief, as a time when the child is without supervision—and hence as a time when a plan for the child's safety is required.

All children need to learn to be responsible for their own safety and behaviour when not being supervised by an adult. Permission to go places and do things in the community unsupervised is a privilege to be earned, not a right. This privilege or responsibility should be given in small steps as the older child or teen demonstrates that he or she is able to manage time or stay out of danger or trouble when outside of adult supervision.

What is the child usually doing just prior to becoming involved with fire?

Children tend to get into trouble (including fire involvement) when they are bored and have nothing better or more exciting to occupy their time.

Engaging children or adolescents in structured activities inside or outside of the home has multiple benefits. Planned activities keep the child busy and out of trouble and leave less opportunity for impulsive acts.

Structured activities are usually skill-building, and many require some self-discipline. They also provide pleasure, excitement and a sense of accomplishment. These are additional benefits for the child.

Who is the child with prior to becoming involved with fire?

Many children become involved in firesetting because they are in the presence of other children, and sometimes adults:

· who are involved with fire

· who are antisocial or

· who influence them to engage in behaviours they are unlikely to engage in when alone.

The link between associating with peers who engage in antisocial behaviour and the committing of antisocial acts is well established.

There is also evidence that exposure to inappropriate fire behaviours of others (be they peers, siblings or caregivers) is specifically linked to inappropriate fire involvement by children.

For obvious reasons, the child should be prohibited and/or discouraged from spending time unsupervised with other children who have ignition sources or with adults who use ignition sources in inappropriate ways. Such individuals are not only poor role models for the child, but they are also likely to afford the child access to ignition materials.

Help the caregiver identify the links between the absence of supervision, and/or the absence of planned activities, and/or the presence of peers who engage in antisocial behaviour and fire involvement.

> *Use the following questions to help the caregiver complete Part 1 of the* Antecedents to Fire Involvement *worksheet. Start with the child's last episode of fire involvement, and then ask about two or three other episodes of fire involvement to gather information about the antecedents to the child's fire involvement.*

- **Where was your child during his or her last episode of fire involvement?**
- **What was your child doing at the time?**
- **Who was your child with?**
- **Where was the caregiver?**

> *Use the caregiver's responses to the questions about antecedents to the child's fire involvement to help the caregiver complete Part 2 of the* Antecedents to Fire Involvement *worksheet. Decide whether or not the following antecedents played a role for each of the child's fire episodes:*

- **Was the absence of adult supervision a factor?**
- **Was the absence of structured or planned activities a factor?**
- **Was the presence of poor role models a factor? (Was the child copying or influenced by someone else?)**

Note: If there have been very few episodes of fire involvement, help the caregiver do this exercise by asking him or her to provide examples of other episodes of misbehaviour by the child.

Plan ahead for times when the child will be without supervision.

Whenever a young child is going to be outside of adult supervision (unable to be seen or heard) even briefly, or when an adolescent is going to be without supervision for a longer period of time, the caregiver should evaluate whether or not the child will be safe and plan ahead to reduce the risk of fire involvement, as appropriate.

We have found that most children and adolescents seem to accept new caregiver behaviours or demands more easily when these are implemented to help keep them safe.

Before the child is permitted to be without supervision, the caregiver should know:

· where the child is going to be

· what the child is going to be doing

· who else is going to be with the child and

· whether access to ignition materials is a concern.

Thinking about these questions will help the caregiver evaluate the child's risk for further fire involvement or, more generally, whether or not the child will be safe and stay out of trouble.

If the caregiver judges that access to fire-starting materials is likely or possible, or that the child will be in the company of others who are not fire-safe, then a plan can be made to deal with this risk.

Obviously, certain environments or situations pose greater risk than others depending on such factors as the child's age and disposition. For example, it may be all right to leave the child unsupervised while he or she is engaged in a planned activity for 10 minutes in the family room—but not in the kitchen. Similarly, it may be all right for an older child to be out in the community unsupervised for four hours to attend a basketball game, but not to "hang out" at the local mall.

These examples illustrate that a supervision or monitoring checklist can be very useful in helping the caregiver, and eventually the child, plan ahead for unsupervised time. For example, if the caregiver is going to leave a younger child unattended for 10 minutes, then some activity to bridge this time can be planned.

For older children, going out into the community on their own can be made contingent on having a plan that addresses any caregiver concerns about the lack of supervision. If the child is not able to provide sufficient information regarding whereabouts, activities and companions in advance, the caregiver and child can negotiate what additional planning needs to occur before the child will be permitted to be in the community without supervision.

Once a plan has been agreed upon, the child can then be made accountable for adhering to the plan, and further privileges involving unsupervised time in the community or loss of such privileges can be made contingent on the child's behaviours. Ideally, running through this type of checklist should become an almost automatic process for the caregiver and eventually for the child.

Ask the following questions to help the caregiver complete the Times without Supervision *worksheet. Practise completing the worksheet questions for three or four different situations that will arise during the upcoming week.*

- **When will your child be unsupervised?**

- **Where is your child going to be?**

- **What is your child going to be doing?**

- **Who, if anyone, is your child going to be with?**

- **Is access to fire-starting materials likely?**

- **Is observation of fire-dangerous behaviour likely?**

- **How long is it reasonable to leave the child with no adult contact?**

- **When should the caregiver and child be in contact by phone or some other means? (check-in time)**

- **What are some things that you, the caregiver, could do that would help insure your child's safety?**

- **What are some things that your child could do that would help ensure safety during times without supervision?**

Wrap-up and joint meeting with caregiver and child

Guidelines: 15 minutes

Provide a brief review of the skills learned in this session. Focus on the efforts and progress of the caregiver and child and provide liberal praise and recognition for these efforts.

If the child has learned SNAP™ and if this was not done in the last session's wrap-up, have the child show the caregiver the steps to SNAP™ and help the child teach the caregiver these steps.

Have the caregiver show the child the *Times without Supervision* worksheet, p. 56, and help the caregiver explain the principles involved.

Have the caregiver inform the child about the other caregivers who will be told about the family's fire-safety practices.

Discuss home practice.

The following are the suggested home practice activities to be completed before the next session:

1. The caregiver and child should conduct the home check for ignition materials and update the previously completed *Home Fire-Safety Search* worksheet, p. 22.

2. Once a day until the next session, the caregiver should sit with the child and plan for times that day or the following day that the child will be out of the caregiver's view or unsupervised. Together they should complete the *Times without Supervision* worksheet.

3. The caregiver should tell others who will be supervising the child about the fire involvement of the child and fire-safety routines that will help.

4. The caregiver should help the child practise SNAP™. Complete two *SNAP™ Tracking Sheets*, p. 162.

5. The caregiver should reward the child for fire-safe behaviours and for using SNAP™.

6. The caregiver and child should use the *Home Practice Checklist*, p. 164, to check off the tasks they have completed.

Optional activity

Using the *Safe Activities* worksheet, the caregiver should make a list with the child of activities that the child can do when unsupervised in the home or when the child is in the community on his or her own. Assign each activity a location and check-in time.

Worksheet

■ Caregiver

Information to Share with Other Caregivers

1. Who should be told?

   e.g., Johnny's grandmother and other care providers

2. What information should be shared?

   e.g., Johnny is very interested in fire and lighters and needs his grandmother's help to avoid the temptation to touch or try using lighters or matches. Please help by locking up all matches and lighters and do not allow Johnny to touch them.

Antecedents to Fire Involvement – Part 1

(Describe the fire situations!)

Situation 1

Where was the child? _e.g., at the park_

What was the child doing? _e.g., hanging out_

Who was the child with? _e.g., friend from school_

How was the child feeling? _e.g., bored_

Where was the caregiver? _e.g., at home_

Situation 2

Where was the child? _____

What was the child doing? _____

Who was the child with? _____

How was the child feeling? _____

Where was the caregiver? _____

Situation 3

Where was the child? _____

What was the child doing? _____

Who was the child with? _____

How was the child feeling? _____

Where was the caregiver? _____

Antecedents to Fire Involvement – Part 2

	Situation 1	Situation 2	Situation 3
Was lack of supervision an issue?			
Was lack of planned activities an issue?			
Was presence of poor role models an issue?			

Times without Supervision

Answer the questions to help plan for times the child will be without supervision:

When will the child be
without supervision? _____

Where will
the child be? _____

What will the
child be doing? _____

Who will be
with the child? _____

Is access to ignition
materials a concern? _____

Check in time: When
should I check in with my child? _____

Things the caregiver can do
to keep the child safe: _____

Things the child can do that
would help keep him- or herself safe: _____

TAPP-C
Worksheet (optional)

▪ Caregiver

Safe Activities

Things my child can do that are safe:

What	Where	For How Long
e.g., attend swimming lessons	e.g., community centre	e.g., 60 minutes

Session **3** **TAPP-C**
Progress Note

▪ Caregiver

Fire Safety Away from Home:
Preventing Situations that Lead to Fire Involvement

Name: _____ File no.: _____ Session date: _____

Action plan:

☐ Client cancelled (specify action plan) _____

☐ No show (specify action plan) _____

☐ Clinician cancelled (specify action plan) _____

☐ Attended Session 3 of the TAPP-C program

Fire involvement since last session? ☐ Yes ☐ No

Fire-safety education: ☐ In progress ☐ Done ☐ Not started ☐ N/A

This session covered the following:

Covered	*Not covered*	
☐	☐	Began with joint meeting/check-in with caregiver and child
☐	☐	Reviewed previous home practice
☐	☐	Discussed importance of sharing fire-specific information with other caregivers
☐	☐	Identified link between absence of supervision, absence of planned activities, antisocial peers and fire involvement
☐	☐	Developed skills in planning ahead for times youth will be without supervision
☐	☐	Ended with joint meeting with caregiver and youth
☐	☐	Discussed home practice

Outcome of session:

☐ Next session scheduled for: _____

☐ Treatment terminated (client initiated)   ☐ Treatment terminated (clinician initiated)

Additional notes:

_____   _____
Signature/Credentials   Date

Consequences of Fire Involvement: What to Do if It Happens Again

Session at a glance

Background

Session 3 focused on the antecedents to children's fire involvement; this session will focus on the role of consequences or what happens after the fire involvement.

Like other behaviours, the child's fire involvement is responsive to the consequences that follow it. While some events (consequences) that follow fire involvement are positive and will increase the probability that the fire involvement will occur again, other consequences are negative and will decrease the probability that the behaviour will occur again.

This session provides the caregiver with the opportunity to discuss the outcomes or consequences of the child's fire involvement. Common but ineffective or maladaptive caregiver responses to a child's fire involvement are reviewed.

Subsequently, the clinician will assist the caregiver to develop a plan for dealing with any future fire involvement by the child. Just as the caregiver learned to plan ahead to prevent high-risk situations or antecedents to the fire involvement, the caregiver can also learn to use consequences effectively to help stop further fire involvement.

Session 4 of the child sessions also focuses on consequences of the child's fire involvement. The child will get additional practice using SNAP™ to stop him- or herself from touching an ignition source and for planning other things to do instead. The emphasis will be on helping the child think about the likely consequences (positive or negative) of his or her choices or plans.

Goals

· Check in with the caregiver and child.

· Review last session's home practice activities with the caregiver and child.

· Identify the positive outcomes associated with fire involvement and generate alternative ways to achieve similar outcomes.

· Identify ineffective consequences.

· Select appropriate consequences.

· Problem-solve to determine what went wrong if another episode occurs.

· Wrap up and review next week's home practice activities with the caregiver and the child.

If short of time

Your main goal is to collaborate with the caregiver in developing a proactive plan to deal with future fire involvement by the child.

Materials needed

· paper

· pencils

· Session 4 worksheets (p. 73)

· Session 4 progress note (p. 79)

Joint meeting with caregiver and child

Guidelines: 15 minutes

Check-in

Have there been any further episodes of fire involvement since the last appointment?

If no further fire involvement is reported by the caregiver or child, assume the best and praise both participants for their efforts and good work.

If further fire involvement has occurred, model for the caregiver and child an appropriate response that includes recognizing the seriousness of this behaviour and the need for problem-solving to determine what went wrong, as well as how to intervene further. (See Clinician Note, p. 65.)

If appropriate, ask the following question:

What is your family's status and progress with the Fire Service Education portion of TAPP-C?

Review of home practice

Review the home practice from Session 3 with the caretaker and the child. Ask the following questions:

Did your family do the home check for ignition materials?

Did you (the caregiver) help the child practise SNAP™?

Did you (the caregiver) tell others who will be supervising the child about the child's fire involvement and about the fire-safety routines that will help?

Did you work together to plan ahead regarding times the child would be without supervision?

Did you use the *Times without Supervision* worksheet?

Did the family reward themselves for fire-safe behaviours?

Did you work together on the *Safe Activities* worksheet (optional) to make a list of activities that the child can do when unsupervised in the home or when in the community on his or her own?

When the family was able to carry out the home practice, ask the following question:

■ **What did the caregiver and the child find helpful about these new home fire-safety activities?**

When the family was unable or unwilling to carry out the home practice, ask the following questions:

■ **What prevented you from carrying out the home practice activities?**

■ **Can you think of ways to overcome these obstacles?**

The clinician should use a collaborative, problem-solving approach to work with the family on how to overcome barriers to completing the home practice activities.

Clinician Note

The agenda for Session 4 should not begin until you are satisfied that the caregiver and child understand the importance of limiting access to incendiaries, monitoring the home for access, and rewarding fire-safe behaviours when they occur.

Caregiver alone

Guidelines: 60 minutes

Identify positive outcomes that the fire involvement may be providing the child, and generate alternative ways to achieve similar outcomes.

Help the caregiver identify any positive outcomes the fire involvement may be bringing the child by completing question 1 of the *Positive Outcomes of Fire Involvement* worksheet.

Ask the following questions:

- Why do some children and teenagers like playing with fire?
- What kind of things happen that make them want to try it again?
- What makes playing with fire positive or pleasurable?
- Is playing with fire exciting?
- Does playing with fire make your child feel powerful?
- Does playing with fire bring your child attention?
- Is there a particular function that being involved with fire might serve for your child?

Engage the caregiver as a collaborator by helping him or her to think of activities or behaviours that could serve the same function(s) as fire involvement. Complete questions 2 to 4 of the *Positive Outcomes of Fire Involvement* worksheet.

Ask the following questions:

- What other safe ways are there for the child to achieve similar outcomes?
- Is there something that you could do to help your child use these other behaviours instead of the fire involvement?

Identify ineffective caregiver consequences or responses to the child's fire involvement.

For many reasons, caregivers often respond to their child's fire involvement in highly emotional and ineffective ways. Some caregivers respond with harsh physical discipline. Other caregivers use scare tactics such as threatening to burn the child or showing the child pictures of burned bodies in a desperate attempt to teach the child about the dangers of fire. There is no evidence that these strategies are effective.

Indeed, it is likely that the child does not experience these types of caregiver responses as educational, even if intended that way, but rather experiences them as abusive (e.g., my caregiver tried to burn me). Also, there is very good evidence that harsh discipline is counterproductive in stopping antisocial behaviour in general.

Another maladaptive type of overreaction shown by some caregivers in response to their child's fire involvement is to become too focused on the child's fire involvement. An example of this might be the caregiver who now insists on sleeping with the child or being with the child all of the time. These types of responses by the caregiver are a concern in cases in which the child may be using the firesetting for the very purpose of getting the attention of a caregiver who is otherwise not as available or attentive.

At the other extreme are caregivers who under-react or provide no consequence or response to their child's fire involvement, either because they believe that the fire itself was a sufficient deterrent to further fire involvement or because they have given up trying to discipline the child, believing that nothing they do works.

Unlike some other oppositional behaviours, it is never appropriate to ignore a child's fire involvement because of the risk of injury associated with a child's fire involvement.

Use some of the following questions to engage the caregiver in identifying consequences for a child's fire involvement that are not *effective. Complete question 1 of the* Responding to Fire Involvement *worksheet.*

- **Do you sometimes use consequences for misbehaviour that are not effective?**

- **Why is yelling and screaming usually not effective?**

- **Why is showing your child pictures of burned objects or bodies usually not effective?**

- **Why is hitting or burning your child not effective? What message would this send to your child?**

- **What about doing nothing or ignoring the behaviour? Would this help? What message would this send to your child?**

Engage the caregiver as a collaborator by generating a list of potentially helpful consequences. Complete question 2 of the Responding to Fire Involvement *worksheet. Ask the following questions:*

- **What kinds of consequences might help a child stop the fire involvement?**

- **What kinds of things can you do when your child breaks an important rule?**

- **What kinds of consequences seemed to work with your child in the past?**

Select appropriate consequences for fire involvement.

In general, effective caregiver consequences are:

· consistent (they occur every time the misbehaviour occurs)

· predictable (they are planned so that the caregiver and child both know what the consequences will be)

· meaningful to the child and

· fit the misbehaviour.

One method to devise an appropriate and logical consequence for the child who has been involved in an episode of fire involvement is to break the situation that led to the fire involvement into its component parts: Where was the child? What was the child doing? Who was with the child? The caregiver can also determine whether there is some aspect of this situation that the child values that is reasonable and possible to withhold.

For example, if the fire involvement happened in the community after school while the child was on his or her way home, a logical consequence would be to not permit the child to return home from school alone for some period of time. Alternatively, if the episode occurred while the child was with a particular peer, an effective consequence might be to not permit the child to accompany that peer without supervision for some period of time.

The caregiver and child may benefit from being reminded that the freedom to be left without adult supervision should be considered a privilege and responsibility to be earned by the child who demonstrates that he or she is capable of handling such situations in a responsible manner.

Clinician Note

One caveat in educating caregivers about logical consequences is the notion that it is not a good idea to withhold from the child opportunities for learning prosocial skills (e.g., hockey or scouting) or opportunities for interacting with prosocial peers or adults as a punishment for an antisocial behaviour.

This is a counterproductive strategy because it deprives the child of the very experiences needed to acquire positive behaviours.

Helping the caregiver to become proactive by developing plans about how to respond to any further fire involvement by the child should help reduce inconsistent, impulsive and inappropriate use of consequences. Planning ahead will also help modulate the caregiver's emotions at a critical time.

Present the following scenario to the caregiver and use the questions that follow to stimulate discussion.

SCENARIO

Johnny is walking home from school. He is happy that he no longer has to take the school bus home with the other kids. He sees a lighter in the park and picks it up to try it. A neighbour happens to spot Johnny and accompanies him home and tells his caregiver about the incident.

- **What kind of consequence could you, the caregiver, select for this incident?**
- **What message would that consequence send to the child?**

The clinician should incorporate this scenario and the consequence generated by the parent (or some other more appropriate example) into a role-play on the delivery of effective consequences. Use the following principles:

1. Label the inappropriate behaviour of the child. Be calm, brief and specific. For example, "Johnny, you touched a lighter on the way home from school today."

2. State the consequence. Be calm, brief and specific. For example, "Because you touched the lighter you will not be allowed to walk home from school on your own."

3. Schedule a later time to discuss and problem-solve the incident with the child. Say something like, "I am upset right now and so are you, but tomorrow when we are both calm, we will have a discussion about what went wrong."

Help the caregiver select another scenario and have the caregiver incorporate it into a role-play on using consequences effectively. Give the caregiver feedback about his or her performance. Reinforce the importance of staying calm, sticking to a plan and not getting into a battle with the child.

Learn to use problem-solving to understand what led to any further fire involvement.

Upon discovering that their child has been playing with fire, most caregivers have the natural urge to immediately tell the child how dangerous fire can be and how vital it is to stop this behaviour. Unfortunately, these admonitions, although well intentioned, are rarely done calmly or in a manner that is likely to result in any learning or benefit to the child.

In the same way that high arousal may prevent the caregiver from disciplining the child in an effective manner, it also precludes effective problem-solving or education about fire safety. In addition, the child who has just been caught firesetting is likely to be frightened or defensive, and not be open to education at that point.

Caregivers should keep their efforts to educate the child separate from their efforts to discipline the child.

After the caregiver has provided a consequence for the fire involvement, he or she should pick a later time to have a discussion with the child about the episode. The discussion should include questions and tactics that encourage the child's problem-solving and collaboration and that focus on what went wrong and how to prevent another occurrence in the future. The following are possible questions for problem-solving why another episode occurred. They are also listed in the Problem-Solving Why Another Episode of Fire Involvement Occurred *worksheet for the caregiver.*

Where did the child get the ignition source for the fire involvement?

What could the child have done to prevent the occurrence?

What could the caregiver have done to prevent the occurrence?

Does anyone else need to be told about the episode to help prevent another occurrence?

Use a continuation of the scenario about Johnny to engage the caregiver in thinking about an episode of fire involvement as an opportunity to problem-solve what went wrong and to review the family's fire-safety practices.

SCENARIO (CONTINUED)

Sometime the next day, Johnny's mother plans for the two of them to sit down and calmly discuss the incident.

- **What should the goal of the discussion between the caregiver and Johnny be?**

- **What kinds of questions should the caregiver ask?**

- **What kind of information does the caregiver need to understand what went wrong?**

- **How can the caregiver get the child to help problem-solve what went wrong?**

- **What kind of message does this joint problem-solving send to the child?**

Given that further fire involvement indicates the re-emergence of fire-dangerous behaviours, it is also an opportune time to review the family's fire-safety behaviours with the goal of revisiting whether they are adequate and still being practised and rewarded. The following questions are helpful in this regard, and are also included in the caregiver's worksheet:

- **Is the *Home Fire-Safety Search* worksheet, p. 22, still posted in a prominent place?**

- **Is the family still practising the fire-safety behaviours?**

- **Is the child still practising SNAP™?**

- **Are varied rewards (praise, tangible rewards) still being provided for using fire-safe behaviours?**

- **What does the family need to do to get back on track with fire safety?**

Wrap-up and joint meeting with caregiver and child

Guidelines: 15 minutes

Have the caregiver and child share their ideas about the functions or positive things the fire involvement may be bringing the child and their ideas about alternative and safer ways of achieving those outcomes. Are there any additional things either the caregiver or the child could do to help achieve these outcomes in more appropriate ways?

Ask the caregiver to explain to the child the way that he or she will be dealing with any future fire involvement. Have the caregiver go through the steps he or she will use. Ask the child's views about the suggested consequences. Does the child have any suggestions regarding consequences that would work for him or her?

Have the child demonstrate the use of SNAP™ and ask him or her to think out loud about the likely consequences of his or her choice of different plans or behaviours (e.g., looking for a lighter versus doing something else). Finish the session by drafting a contract stating that the child has agreed that he or she will no longer play with fire, and describing the agreed upon consequences for any further fire involvement. Have the caregiver and child sign the contract and witness them signing it. (Refer to *Contract*.)

Discuss home practice.

The following are the suggested home practice activities to be completed before the next session:

1. The caregiver should post the *Contract* in an obvious place in the home, such as on the door of the fridge.

2. The caregiver and child should check the home for ignition materials and update the *Home Fire Safety Search* worksheet, p. 22.

3. The caregiver should help the child practise SNAP™ on two occasions: one on paper (see the *SNAP™ Tracking* worksheet, p. 183) and one through a role-play focusing on identifying choices and consequences. The caregiver and child can also discuss how SNAP™ can be used for any situations that have occurred or will likely occur before the next session. The caregiver should sign off on this home practice activity.

4. Once a day until the next session, the caregiver should sit with the child and plan for times that day or the following day that the child will be unsupervised or out of the caregiver's view. Together they should complete the *Times without Supervision* worksheet, p. 185.

5. The caregiver should reward the child for fire-safe behaviours.

6. The caregiver should help the child complete the Home Practice Checklist, p. 186, by checking off the tasks the child has finished.

Positive Outcomes of Fire Involvement

1. Things my child likes about the fire involvement:

   e.g., excitement, peer recognition, attention from family

2. Safe ways to get similar outcomes:

   e.g., play basketball, build a skill that peers admire, set times to be with child

3. Things caregiver can do to help:

   e.g., find local basketball courts and buy/borrow a basketball,
   play basketball with child.

4. Things child can do to help:

   e.g., talk with mom when problems with peers arise,
   find pick-up basketball game.

TAPP-C
Worksheet

Caregiver

Responding to Fire Involvement

1. Consequences of Fire Involvement that Do Not Help

   e.g., yelling, crying, threatening to burn/show burned objects, doing nothing.

   Help the caregiver list consequences of fire involvement that weren't helpful.

2. Effective Consequences of Fire Involvement

   e.g., Remove privilege of being in community without supervision.

   Help the caregiver list consequences of fire involvement that were helpful.

Problem-Solving Why Another Episode of Fire Involvement Occurred

1. Where did the child get the ignition source for the fire involvement? _____

2. What could the child have done to prevent the occurrence? _____

3. What could the parent have done to prevent the occurrence? _____

4. Does anyone else need to be told about the episode to help prevent another occurrence? _____

5. Is the *Home Fire-Safety Search* worksheet still posted? _____

6. Is the family still practising the fire-safety behaviours? _____

7. Is the child still practicing SNAP™? _____

8. Are rewards still being provided for using fire-safe behaviours? _____

9. What does the family need to do to get back on track with fire safety? _____

Contract

Date: _____

I, _____ ,
promise that I will no longer touch matches,
lighters or anything else that could start a fire.

If I break my promise, my _____
(mother, father, etc.) will choose a consequence
for me from the list we have agreed on.

Signed,

Child: _____

Caregiver: _____

Witness: _____

TAPP-C

Worksheet

Caregiver

Times without Supervision

Answer the questions to help plan for times the child will be without supervision:

When will the child be
without supervision? _____

Where will
the child be? _____

What will the
child be doing? _____

Who will be
with the child? _____

Is access to ignition
materials a concern? _____

Check in time: When
should I check in with my child? _____

Things the caregiver can do
to keep the child safe: _____

Things the child can do that
would help keep him- or herself safe: _____

TAPP-C
Progress Note

Caregiver

Consequences of Fire Involvement:
What to Do if It Happens Again

Name: _____   File no.: _____   Session date: _____

Action plan:

☐ Client cancelled (specify action plan)   _____

☐ No show (specify action plan)   _____

☐ Clinician cancelled (specify action plan)   _____

☐ Attended Session 4 of the TAPP-C program

Fire involvement since last session?   ☐ Yes   ☐ No

Fire-safety education: ☐ In progress   ☐ Done   ☐ Not started   ☐ N/A

This session covered the following:

Covered	*Not covered*	
☐	☐	Began with joint meeting/check-in with caregiver and child
☐	☐	Reviewed previous home practice
☐	☐	Reviewed any positive outcomes of fire involvement and generated alternative ways to achieve similar outcomes
☐	☐	Reviewed ineffective consequences to fire involvement
☐	☐	Reviewed characteristics of effective consequences
☐	☐	Discussed selecting appropriate consequences
☐	☐	Discussed using problem-solving to understand new episodes of fire involvement
☐	☐	Ended with joint meeting with caregiver and child
☐	☐	Discussed home practice

Outcome of session:

☐ Next session scheduled for: _____

☐ Treatment terminated (client initiated)   ☐ Treatment terminated (clinician initiated)

Additional notes:

_____   _____
Signature/Credentials   Date

Termination: Reviewing Fire-Safe Behaviours and Recognizing the Caregiver's Accomplishments

Session at a glance

Background

The final session provides an opportunity to review the issues covered and progress made in the previous sessions, and to develop a relapse prevention plan should fire involvement re-occur. It also provides an opportunity to

· discuss the termination of the TAPP-C intervention

· formally recognize the completion of the TAPP-C program

· discuss any further interventions that are recommended for the child and/or family.

Goals

· Check in with the caregiver and child.

· Review last session's home practice activity with the caregiver and child.

· Discuss termination issues.

· Review progress made.

· Develop a relapse prevention plan.

· Meet with the caregiver and child to review the main points of the treatment intervention, as well as to discuss any further interventions that are recommended.

· Recognize the completion of the TAPP-C program.

If short of time

Your main goals are to discuss termination issues, to review the proactive plans to prevent future fire involvement, and to facilitate any referrals for ongoing or supplemental treatment.

Materials needed

· paper

· pencils

· *Certificate of Completion* worksheet (p. 91)

· consent forms to contact other agencies, if necessary

· Session 5 progress note (p. 93)

Joint meeting with caregiver and child

Guidelines: 15 minutes

Check-in

* **Have there been any further episodes of fire involvement since the last appointment?**

If no further fire involvement is reported by the caregiver or child, assume the best and praise both participants for their efforts and good work.

If further fire involvement has occurred, model for the caregiver and child an appropriate response that includes recognizing the seriousness of this behaviour and the need for problem-solving to determine what went wrong, as well as how to intervene further.

Clinician Note

Termination is usually dependent on feeling comfortable that the child's fire involvement has stopped. Obviously, the clinician will need to think very carefully about terminating with a family if the child is still engaging in fire involvement.

If appropriate, ask the following question:

* **What is your family's status and progress with the Fire Service Education portion of TAPP-C?**

Review of home practice

Review the home practice from Session 4 with the caregiver and child.

Ask the following questions:

- **Did the family post the *Contract* (p. 76)?**

- **Did the family search the home for ignition materials?**

- **Is the family keeping ignition materials in the agreed upon ways?**

- **Did the caregiver help the child practise SNAP™?**

- **Did the family plan ahead for times without supervision?**

- **Did the family reward themselves for using the fire-safety behaviours?**

When the family was able to carry out the home practice, ask the following question:

- **What did the caregiver and child find helpful about these new home fire-safety activities?**

Have them talk about these behaviours so that they may become more aware of their usefulness. Be generous with your compliments for a job well done.

If the family was unable or unwilling to carry out the home practice, ask the following questions:

- **What prevented you from carrying out the home practice activities?**

- **Can you think of ways to overcome these obstacles?**

The clinician should use a collaborative, problem-solving approach to working with the family on how to complete the home practice activities. Remind participants that keeping matches, lighters and other ignition sources away from the child is the single most important and probably the easiest step that they can take to stop the child's fire involvement.

Caregiver alone

Guidelines: 60 minutes

Discuss termination issues.

For most caregivers, this will be the last face-to-face intervention session. Other caregivers may require further weekly sessions or periodic booster sessions in order to continue skill development and practice.

If this is the final session, ask the caregiver how he or she is feeling about finishing up. Modify the discussion depending on how the caregiver is thinking and feeling about termination (e.g., some caregivers may feel sad, while others will be more than happy to conclude their sessions).

Regardless of the caregiver's reaction to the final session, the clinician should continue to communicate warmth and acceptance, to show recognition for the caregiver's efforts, and to reinforce any positive changes that have taken place. For example, let the caregiver know that you enjoyed working with him or her.

Communicate your own feelings about the final session; for example, that you are happy that the caregiver has learned some new skills. Be specific with your praise regarding the caregiver's progress to date, highlighting occasions when the caregiver exhibited notable effort or mastered specific fire-safe behaviours or strategies.

Answer any questions or concerns that the caregiver may have regarding termination.

While discussing termination issues, be sure to tell the caregiver to expect a one-month follow-up phone call. (See Clinician Note, p. 88.) Explain that phone contact is a good way for you to monitor progress and to work together regarding any further problem-solving, if necessary.

Also, inform the caregiver that you will give your office phone number to him or her so that the caregiver and/or child can reach you in the future with any questions or concerns.

Review progress.

Briefly review with the caregiver his or her general progress over the course of the intervention. Ask the caregiver's ideas, thoughts and feelings with regard to the following topics:

· the main lessons of the sessions to date

· the perceived strengths and/or areas in need of improvement

· the strategies that seemed to work best

- the situations in the future where the caregiver may have to use his or her new strategies or skills and

- any obstacles to using the new fire-safety strategies and behaviours.

Once the clinician has gained an understanding of the caregiver's perceptions, this can easily lead into a follow-up discussion around these topics. Does the clinician have anything to add with regard to strengths, coping strategies, high risk situations or obstacles?

Make a plan to deal with high-risk situations and firesetting urges that may arise in the future.

At this stage of the intervention, the caregiver should be able to identify the antecedents to the child's fire involvement. As well, the caregiver will have learned and practised a variety of fire-safety strategies and behaviours devised to reduce risks for further fire involvement.

The clinician will need to use this information to help the caregiver articulate a plan to manage risk for further fire involvement. Because the content of this plan will vary depending on the presenting issues of each child, future planning will probably take some combination of clinical judgment and creativity in order to develop a plan that works best for the caregiver and child.

While developing this plan with the caregiver, keep in mind that the overriding goal is to maximize treatment effects; that is, the maintenance of any positive changes that may have resulted from participating in TAPP-C.

Empirical work targeting juveniles who set fires indicates that recidivism is quite common. Therefore, in developing a relapse prevention plan with the caregiver, the clinician will want to normalize any future difficulties that the child may have in terms of applying fire-safe behaviours and skills in real-life situations. For example, the clinician might explain to a caregiver that the child's urges and/or precipitants likely will not "go away overnight." Instead, communicate that it is a matter of managing children's access to fire materials and opportunity to be involved with fire, as well as helping children to manage their urges using the skills they have learned.

Let the caregiver know that, although it may seem tough now, using these strategies and skills will probably come more naturally over time and with lots of practice.

Remind the caregiver that someone has been working with the child and that fire safety is a family issue: both the caregiver and the child will need to continue to work together. The important message that the caregiver should take home is that the strategies that he or she has learned and the skills that the child has learned take time to perfect, as well as a great deal of practice and support from others.

The following are some questions that the clinician might ask the caregiver in the discussion around monitoring and prevention of further fire involvement by the child:

- In your opinion, how likely is it that your child will become reinvolved with fire in the future (e.g., play with matches and/or lighters and/or start a fire)?

- What would be the signs that your child may be heading for reinvolvement with fire?

- Are there any particular stressors that may make your child vulnerable to reinvolvement with fire?

- Where is your child likely to be when he or she becomes involved with fire, and who would he or she be with? When would this reinvolvement likely occur?

- What feelings is your child likely to have prior to becoming involved with fire?

- In what situations are you most likely to have difficulty continuing with the strategies you have been using to help prevent your child's fire involvement?

- What are your options once you realize your child is again at risk for becoming involved with fire?

- What strategies can you use to stop your child from again becoming involved with fire?

- With whom can you talk if you need help in reducing your child's risk for reinvolvement with fire?

- If your child were to become involved with fire in the future, what type of consequences would you use with your child?

At this point in the intervention, the clinician should have identified other service systems involved or needed to co-ordinate treatment planning (e.g., the school, other mental health agencies, child welfare agency and/or local fire department).

For many children, recommendations for further mental health involvement will be part of their treatment plan (e.g., further parent management training programs, psychoeducational assessment, individual or family therapy or community involvement).

When making these recommendations to the caregiver, explore how the caregiver may be assisted in following through with pertinent referrals and offer to facilitate the referral process. The clinician should use his or her clinical judgment as to whether it is appropriate to follow up with the caregiver on these issues with the child present.

Clinician Note

For several years we have been contacting caregivers by telephone one month after they complete the treatment component of TAPP-C.

Most importantly, we use this brief telephone contact to identify children for whom fire involvement has resurfaced and to problem-solve with the caregiver to determine what needs to happen next. For some families, additional sessions with the TAPP-C clinician may be warranted.

We also use this contact to ensure that families are pursuing any of the other mental health recommendations that may have resulted from the TAPP-C risk assessment.

Finally, we use this contact as an opportunity to remind caregivers about the importance of family fire safety and to briefly review the strategies they have obviously been using successfully to keep their child from being reinvolved with fire.

This contact also provides an opportune time to further reinforce the child's efforts at fire safety. For instance, one agency has been sending a one-month letter of congratulations to children who have not had any further fire involvement.

Wrap-up and joint meeting with caregiver and child

Guidelines: 15 minutes

Assist the caregiver and the child in reviewing their plans to help prevent future fire involvement by the child. Ensure that the roles and responsibilities of both the caregiver and child are clear and that the caregiver will be able to provide adequate assistance and support—including rewards—for the child's ongoing efforts.

Discuss recommendations for additional treatment components (e.g., individual, CBT, PMT).

If the child has a commercial, song, poem, story or picture he or she created in the sessions, help the child share it with the caregiver. Discuss the child's accomplishments and the caregiver's accomplishments.

To recognize the child's accomplishments, present the child with a reward that he or she has earned. The reward may be a certificate or a standard item or gift that the clinician uses with all clients, or it may be a reward specifically tailored to that child. For instance, the reward may be something tangible or intangible that has been decided on in advance in consultation with the caregiver.

Present the family with a *Certificate of Completion.*

Clinician Note

Regardless of the length and manner of celebration, be sure to thank the caregiver for his or her help and support and to communicate to the child how pleased you are with his or her efforts and accomplishments.

Certificate of Completion

For hard work and effort at becoming fire-safe

Names of participants:

_____

_____

Date: _____

Program representative signature:

_____

5

■ Caregiver

Termination:
Reviewing Fire-Safe Behaviours and
Recognizing the Caregiver's Accomplishments

Name: _____ File no.: _____ Session date: _____

Action plan:

☐ Client cancelled (specify action plan)　　_____

☐ No show (specify action plan)　　　　　　_____

☐ Clinician cancelled (specify action plan)　_____

☐ Attended Session 5 of the TAPP-C program

Fire involvement since last session?　　☐ Yes　　☐ No

Fire-safety education:　　☐ In progress　　☐ Done　　☐ Not started　　☐ N/A

This session covered the following:

Covered	*Not covered*	
☐	☐	Began with joint meeting/check-in with caregiver and child
☐	☐	Reviewed previous home practice
☐	☐	Discussed termination issues
☐	☐	Reviewed progress over course of intervention
☐	☐	Planned for management of future risks
☐	☐	Ended with joint meeting with caregiver and child
☐	☐	Presented Certificate or reward

Additional notes:

_____　　_____
Signature/Credentials　　　　　　　　　　Date

Part 3

Child Treatment Sessions

TAPP-C

Fire Safety Begins at Home: Defining and Rewarding Fire-Safe Behaviour

Session at a glance

Background

This session focuses on the importance of family fire safety and the efforts that the child can make to help.

In this session, the child will begin to learn about the importance of replacing his or her fire-dangerous behaviours with fire-safe behaviours. Initially, there will be a joint meeting with the caregiver and child to develop and clarify fire-safety goals for the family. This will set the stage for a "team approach" to fire safety.

Throughout the session, the child will learn and practise new skills to increase fire-safe practices in the home. For instance, he or she will learn the importance of appropriate rules for the use of matches and lighters and the central role of access prevention. The child will identify and practise various strategies to help the caregiver control ignition sources within the home. As well, the child will learn about the opportunity for family rewards for positive gains toward fire safety in the home.

The caregiver's session closely parallels the child's session and highlights the central role of the caregiver in promoting fire-safety practices within the home. Through the caregiver's completion of the *Family Safety Rules for Ignition Materials,* p. 21 and *Home Fire-Safety Search* worksheets, the caregiver and the child will begin to work on developing and communicating explicit rules about the use of fire-starting materials for all members of the family. Child worksheets, which follow each session, can be used individually or put together to form a Fire-Safety Practice Book.

Goals

· Joint meeting: Discuss the main goals of the intervention and briefly describe the program to the child and caregiver.

· Begin to establish rapport with the child through the introductory exercises.

· Help the child to develop an understanding of why it is important to address fire involvement.

· Engage the child as a collaborator in home fire safety; get the child on board to support the caregiver's efforts to establish control over ignition materials in the home.

· Help build skills on how to search the home for ignition sources and where to store ignition materials.

· Wrap up with a joint meeting with the child and caregiver to discuss the session, the home practice activities and the completion rewards.

If short of time:

Your main goals are to begin establishing a therapeutic alliance with the child and to get the child on board with the goal of increasing fire-safe behaviours and eliminating fire-dangerous behaviours.

Materials needed

· blank white paper

· pencils

· coloured markers or pencil crayons

· Session 1 practice worksheets (p. 109)

· stickers or other incentives

· Session 1 progress note (p. 119)

Joint meeting with child and caregiver

Guidelines: 15 minutes

Describe the intervention program.

Why is the family here?

Ensure that the child and caregiver understand that they are here because of the child's involvement with matches, lighters, fire play and/or firesetting. Highlight the fact that this is a very *dangerous* behaviour that puts the whole family at risk for burn injury and that TAPP-C is a family fire-safety and injury prevention program.

Clinicians need to be aware of the reporting requirements specific to their professional organization and jurisdiction. For further information on fire-specific reporting issues, please refer to the Special Issues section on Child Welfare, p. 209.

Clinician Note

At the beginning of each session, the limits of confidentiality should be reviewed, and the child and caregiver should be asked whether there have been any other episodes of fire involvement since the previous session.

This may seem counterintuitive, as the child may be less likely to self-report further fire involvement with the knowledge that the clinician can't "keep this a secret" and must deal with the issue.

However, clear, honest and consistent communication about the clinician's role and responsibilities may ultimately save the therapeutic relationship by preventing misunderstandings down the road about what the clinician can and cannot do.

What is the goal?

Describe the overall goal as working together to make sure that the child stays safe from fire.

How do we do this? As a team, the caregiver, child and clinician will work together to ensure that the child stops the fire involvement and increases fire-safe behaviours.

Throughout the intervention sessions, the clinician may often need to reframe the child's fire involvement from a "psychopathology" issue to a "safety" issue. As well, because so many of these children have a history of experiencing negative consequences to a wide range of problematic behaviours, many children will also respond to the idea that this program is meant to help keep them not only safe, but also out of trouble. For instance, the clinician might ask the following question:

Wouldn't it be nice *not* to have your caregiver mad at you for your fire-play/firesetting? *OR* Wouldn't it be nice to stay out of trouble? (The clinician can also highlight other salient issues here.)

How could we reach the goal?

Discuss with the child and caregiver what the intervention process will look like. Be sure to incorporate the ideas of the child and caregiver whenever possible. Include the following points in your discussion:

· There will be five sessions, on average.

· Each session will last about 90 minutes.

· There will be various types of activities for the child; for example, videos, role-playing, workbook tasks and home practice activities for developing new skills.

· Participants will be working as a team with each other and the clinician, and there will be new skill development for the caregiver and child.

· The caregiver, child and treatment team will all be involved and they all have responsibilities. For example, the child and the caregiver will be meeting with the clinician weekly for the next several weeks, and each participant will have take-home practice activities to complete each week and bring back for the next session.

· There will be rewards given in the sessions for co-operation and effort and at home for fire-safe behaviours. These rewards—to be agreed on with the caregiver—can include social incentives such as praise and time with the caregiver, as well as tangible items such as stickers, food or small prizes.

Clinician Note

While it is important to establish a safe environment for everyone to share, it will also be important to convey to the child that everyone (caregiver, child and clinician) is working as a team and that certain secrets can't be kept from the team.

For instance, because fire involvement is such a dangerous behaviour, any information told to the clinician about a fire-related incident will need to be passed on to the caregiver and treatment team.

As part of making the covert behaviour overt, ideally, the child should not be punished if he or she discloses a *previously unknown* fire-related incident, and the clinician should ensure that the caregiver agrees with these parameters.

However, the child needs to be aware that he or she will be working with the clinician and caregiver to establish a proactive plan (including consequences) to deal with any fire involvement from that time on.

After the proactive plan and appropriate consequences have been agreed on, the child will know exactly what consequences to expect should he or she become involved in subsequent fire-related activity.

Child alone
Begin to establish a therapeutic relationship with the child.
Guidelines: 20 minutes

The therapeutic relationship is an integral component of any intervention program, as it builds a foundation for the collaborative work that needs to be done.

Through both verbal and non-verbal communication, the clinician should set a tone of warmth, empathy and genuineness. The ultimate aim is to get the child engaged in the therapeutic process and to promote a safe and supportive environment in which to share his or her thoughts and feelings, as well as to learn new skills.

In many cases, rapport-building may have already begun during an initial assessment process. Some children will be comfortable with the clinician after participating in informal "getting-to-know-you" activities, questionnaires and clinical interviewing. Others will take longer to warm up.

"Getting-to-know-you" exercises can be tailored to the child's individual needs and preferences. Age, developmental level, cognitive ability, and interests and/or hobbies should be taken into account when thinking about this exercise and subsequent activities. For example, younger children may be encouraged to draw pictures with the clinician of their favourite person, hobby, animal or pet.

To get to know an older child, the clinician may wish to discuss with the child favourite music, hobbies, activities, a best friend, top three wishes or any other topics of interest. Depending on the child, something as informal as a word game or paper-and-pencil game may be the best icebreaker.

The clinician may wish to make use of activities that involve teamwork in which both the clinician and child are working together to accomplish a common goal. The clinician may also wish to have the child colour and complete the cover page of the Fire-Safety Practice Book. Discuss with the child the opportunities to earn stickers and rewards in session for his or her efforts. Help the child complete the *Stickers and Rewards: What I Can Earn In Session* worksheet.

Help the child to develop a solid understanding of the importance of learning fire-safe behaviours to replace fire-dangerous behaviours.

Guidelines: 5–10 minutes

Help the child make a list of reasons why it is important to learn fire-safe behaviours to replace fire-dangerous behaviours. Have the child complete the *Reasons Why it Is Important to Learn Fire-Safe Behaviours* worksheet.

The purpose of this exercise is to establish a framework for the more active treatment component. The bottom line for every child is that any type of fire involvement is *dangerous* and *unpredictable*.

The clinician should discuss any ideas provided by the child, reinforce accurate information, and provide new ideas that were not included in the child's original list. The following are some examples that highlight the importance of stopping the child's fire involvement:

Risk of injury to self and others

· Injury is the leading cause of death for all children and adolescents.

· Many children are injured every year because of their involvement with fire.

· Younger children are particularly vulnerable to burn injury related to fire play.

· Fire involvement is one of the leading causes of death for young children.

Damage to property (one's own and others')

· Children playing with fire cause millions of dollars in property damages.

· Children playing with fire most often cause damage to their own property and/or home.

Intent does not equal outcome

· Most children who cause property damage, injuries and/or deaths do not mean to do so.

· The more times a child plays with matches, the more likely it is for an unintentional fire to start.

Omnipotence

· Most children who have accidentally hurt themselves or others thought that they had control over the fire.

Criminal liabilities

· The more times a child plays with matches, the more likely it is that he or she will get caught.

· Starting a fire is a criminal act in Ontario if the child is 12 years of age or older.

· If you are caught with a lighter in your possession, the police are more likely to presume it was you that started a fire in the vicinity.

Use the following questions to begin a discussion with the child about reasons to stop fire involvement:

Why is it important to help children who have been involved with fire-dangerous behaviours?

Why is it important to stop fire involvement?

What could happen if this wasn't stopped?

Why is it important for children to learn fire-safe behaviours?

Get the child on board to support caregiver rules about the use and storage of ignition materials.

Guidelines: 15–20 minutes

The goal of this portion of the session is to help the child understand that family fire-safe behaviours include explicit rules about the child's use of ignition sources and explicit rules about caregiver control over the child's access to matches, lighters and other ignition sources in the home.

The child should be made aware that the clinician is working with the caregivers on establishing these basic fire-safe behaviours.

For safety reasons, it is recommended that young children never be allowed to touch matches, lighters or other ignition sources. Older children should only be allowed to touch ignition sources and flammables with permission or supervision, as negotiated with the caregiver. All ignition sources should be kept in a secure—locked—place. If working with younger children (e.g., preschoolers) or with adolescents, please see the Special Issues sections on these age groups, p. 206 and p. 207.

Use the following questions to begin a discussion with the child about why families should have rules about who uses ignition sources and where ignition sources should be kept. The questions should also help the child understand the link between access to ignition materials and fire involvement. Have the child complete the Rules about Ignition Materials in the Home *worksheet.*

- Does your family have rules about the use of ignition sources? For example, are there any rules about the use of matches or lighters in your home?

- Are the rules different for adults versus children in your home? Why or why not?

- Should you be permitted to use matches or lighters? Why or why not?

- Do most homes have these types of rules?

- Why are these types of rules important?

- What are the advantages of storing matches and lighters in a secure way?

- Does being able to get matches or lighters sometimes lead kids to use them?

Plan a search of the home for ignition materials and/or accelerants.

Guidelines: 15–20 minutes

Use the following questions to generate discussion about how the family can get rid of all unnecessary fire-starting materials:

- Do you know where there are ignition sources and/or accelerants in your home?

- Where is the most likely place that matches or lighters or accelerants would be found?

- How could your family get rid of any unnecessary matches, lighters and/or accelerants?

- How could you help?

- How could your caregiver help?

Once the child has gained some understanding as to why rules and access are important issues for the family's fire safety, the clinician can develop and practise a plan with the child so that he or she will help the caregiver check for access to ignition sources within the home by conducting a room-by-room search of the house. If the child is residing in a group home or residential facility, please refer to the Special Issues section on Group Homes and Residential Facilities, p. 205.

Clinician Note:

In our experience, children are often better informants than their caregivers with regard to the location of ignition sources and/or accelerants within the home. Many children and teens know exactly where to find matches, lighters or other ignition sources that caregivers thought were well hidden or inaccessible.

In addition, many children keep their own stash of fire-starting materials hidden from the caregiver.

Inform the child that "kids are sometimes the best at knowing where to find matches and lighters and other ignition materials at home" and that "we want to let your caregiver know where the matches and lighters are so that we can work as a team to keep the family safe."

Remind the child that he or she will not get into any trouble at this point, even if he or she tells the clinician and caregiver about a hidden stash of ignition sources. Use the *Home Map* worksheet to help the child highlight with pencils or markers the most likely places to find ignition sources. This often provides a good indication of where the access monitoring can begin. For children who are seldom good at anything and often get into trouble, this is an opportunity to be good at something and earn praise and a reward for their help.

For instance, have the child identify the most likely places in the home where incendiary materials are located, stored or hidden. Have the child mark an "X" in all locations that require checking with the caregiver as the home practice activity.

Inform the child that he or she will be sharing the *Home Map* worksheet with the caregiver during the joint meeting. Note that the child and caregiver will be taking this map home with them to check all the identified areas (as well as other areas in the home) for ignition sources so that the caregiver can eliminate the child's access to fire materials in the home.

Explain that the search will be conducted by the child and caregiver together to ensure that long-forgotten ignition sources are found and destroyed or locked away.

The notion of teamwork can be emphasized here. The clinician may wish to do a role-play of the caregiver conducting a search of the home with the child. Prepare together for this scenario. For example, have the child pretend that he or she has discovered matches or a lighter lying somewhere around the house. Role-play the caregiver and take the scenario to its conclusion.

Give feedback to the child on the exercise. Anticipate difficulties and problem-solve around potential impediments for the child. Ensure that the child knows what to do (e.g., who to tell) if he or she sees ignition sources within the home.

While developing a plan with the child, be sure to address the child's role versus the caregiver's role. For example, "Because we don't want you to ever touch matches or lighters, searches should only be done with your caregiver."

Review this to ensure that the child understands the home practice activity. Make certain that the child knows that (1) this search is only done in the home with the caregiver present, and (2) if he or she happens to come upon an ignition source inside or outside the home, not to touch it, but instead to tell an adult or leave it.

Be sure to praise the child's efforts during the session. If there is time, it is a good idea to end the session with a fun exercise together (e.g., sharing a story or an activity, telling a joke).

Clinician Note:

The clinician should remember not to generate or introduce new fire-related information to the child that could be misused.

For example, if the child has no experience playing with flammables, it may be best to not raise this issue with him or her, as it will be covered in the caregiver's session.

However, if use of flammables is clearly a problem for a particular child, the clinician may wish to have the child generate a list of flammables in the home (e.g., hairspray, lighter fluid, gasoline) and have the child identify locations in the home that should be checked for unsecured accelerants.

The issue of access prevention becomes more difficult in homes in which there is a smoker (e.g., a caregiver or sibling) or in cases in which the child smokes. These issues are dealt with more fully in Session 2, p. 121, and in the Special Issues section on Adolescents, p. 207.

Wrap-up and joint meeting with child and caregiver

Guidelines: 15 minutes

Provide a brief review of the content of the session and the *Family Safety Rules for Ignition Materials,* p. 21, and *Home Fire-Safety Search,* p. 22, worksheets.

Focus on co-operation and efforts of the child and caregiver and provide reinforcement (e.g., verbal praise and recognition) for these efforts at becoming fire-safe. Review the child's *Home Map* worksheet and share and problem-solve solutions to any of the anticipated difficulties noted by the child or caregiver in completing the home practice activities.

Have the child practise telling other family members about what he or she learned and about the goal of the Home Fire-Safety Search.

Have the child and caregiver discuss potential times to do the home search and, if time permits, have the child and caregiver practise by role-playing a room search together.

Discuss the prize, stickers or social incentives that the child and family will be able to earn if the home practice activities are completed. Have the child and caregiver together complete the *Stickers and Rewards: What I Can Earn at Home* worksheet, p. 117.

Discuss home practice.

The following are the suggested home practice activities to be completed before the next session.

1. The caregiver and child should talk to other family members about the importance of family fire-safety practices and the purpose of the home fire-safety search.

2. The caregiver should post the *Home Fire-Safety Search* worksheet, p. 22, in a prominent place at home and use it to track the fire-safety search activities.

Clinician Note:

The clinician should keep a copy of this *Home Fire-Safety Search* worksheet in the family's file for subsequent sessions.

3. The caregiver and child should complete a search of the home, and the caregiver should destroy all unnecessary ignition materials and/or accelerants and lock up those that are kept.

4. With the help of his or her caregiver, the child should complete the *Home Practice Checklist,* p. 118, to check off the tasks completed.

5. The family members should reward themselves for searching the home for ignition materials and for finding an appropriate place to lock up necessary ignition materials and/or accelerants.

TAPP-C
Fire Safety
Practice Book

This Fire Safety Practice Book belongs to...

Name: _____

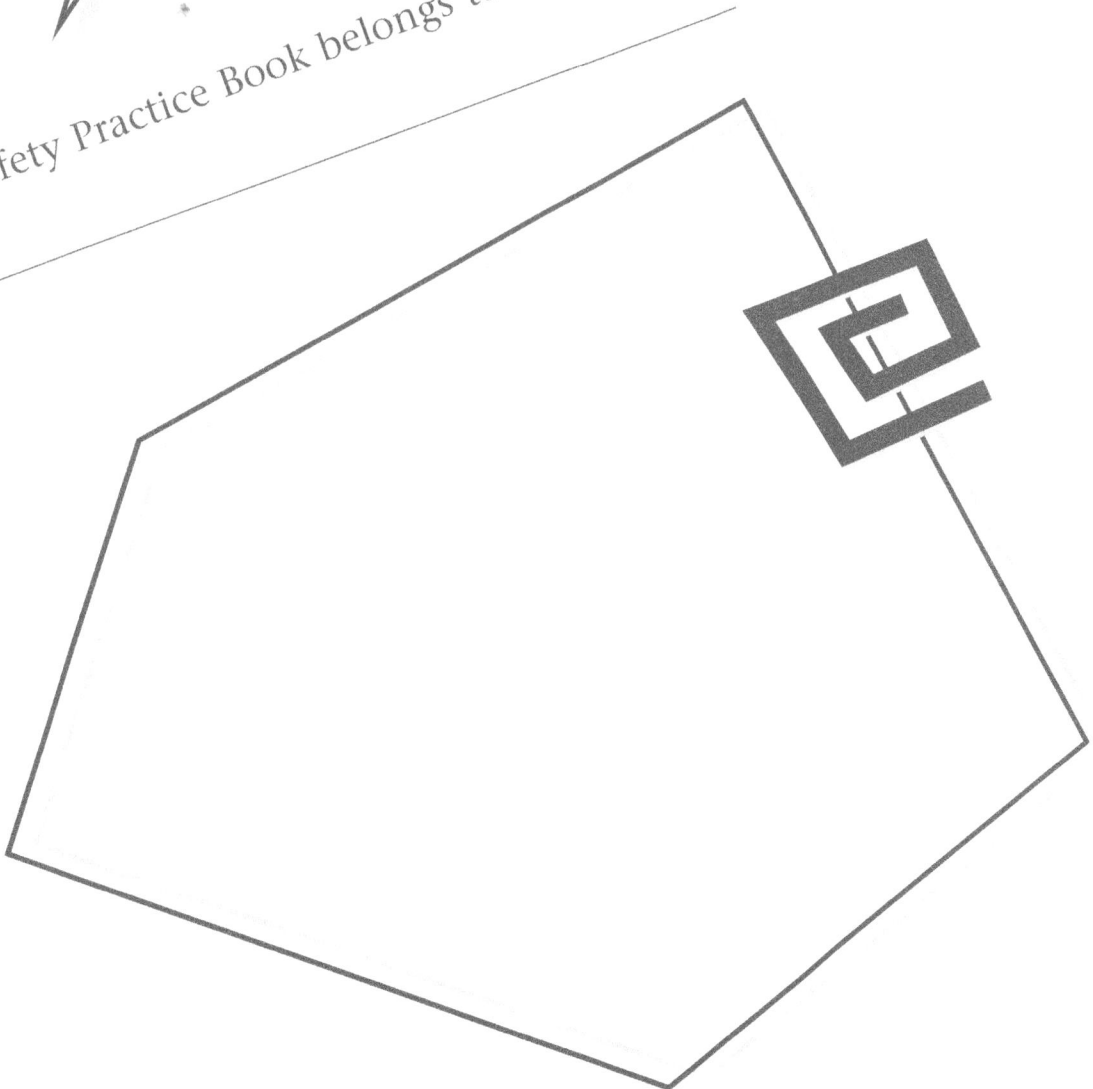

Fire Safety Begins at Home:
Defining and Rewarding Fire-Safe Behaviour

Date: _____

Stickers and Rewards:
What I Can Earn in Session

You can earn stickers in the following ways:

⇨ by bringing the *Fire Safety Practice Book* to your session

⇨ by participating in session

⇨ by working on your home practice activities.

You can earn up to __ stickers at each meeting.
Then, your stickers can be used to earn rewards!

Sticker record

Session 1 ☆

Session 2 ☆

Session 3 ☆

Session 4 ☆

Session 5 ☆

Possible Rewards

 Reward #1

 Reward #2

 Reward #3

 Reward #4

 Reward #5

 Reward #6

Reasons Why It Is Important to Learn Fire-Safe Behaviours

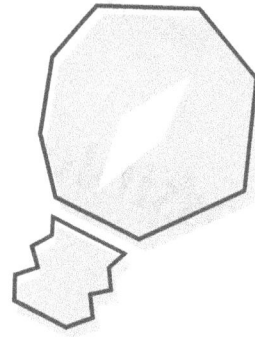

1)

2)

3)

4)

5)

Rules About Ignition Materials in the Home

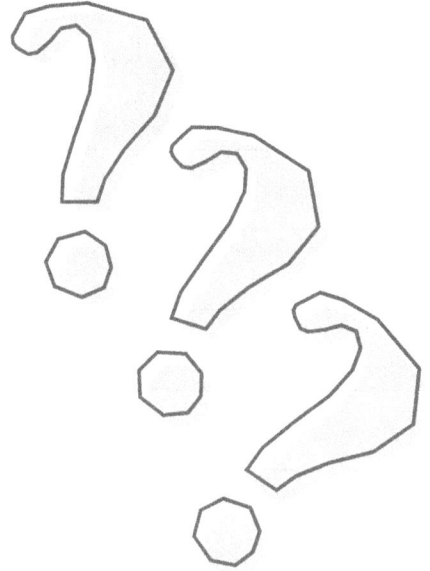

Who is allowed to touch matches and lighters?

Where could matches and lighters be stored safely?

Home Map

Where to check for ignition materials:

1. _____

2. _____

3. _____

4. _____

5. _____

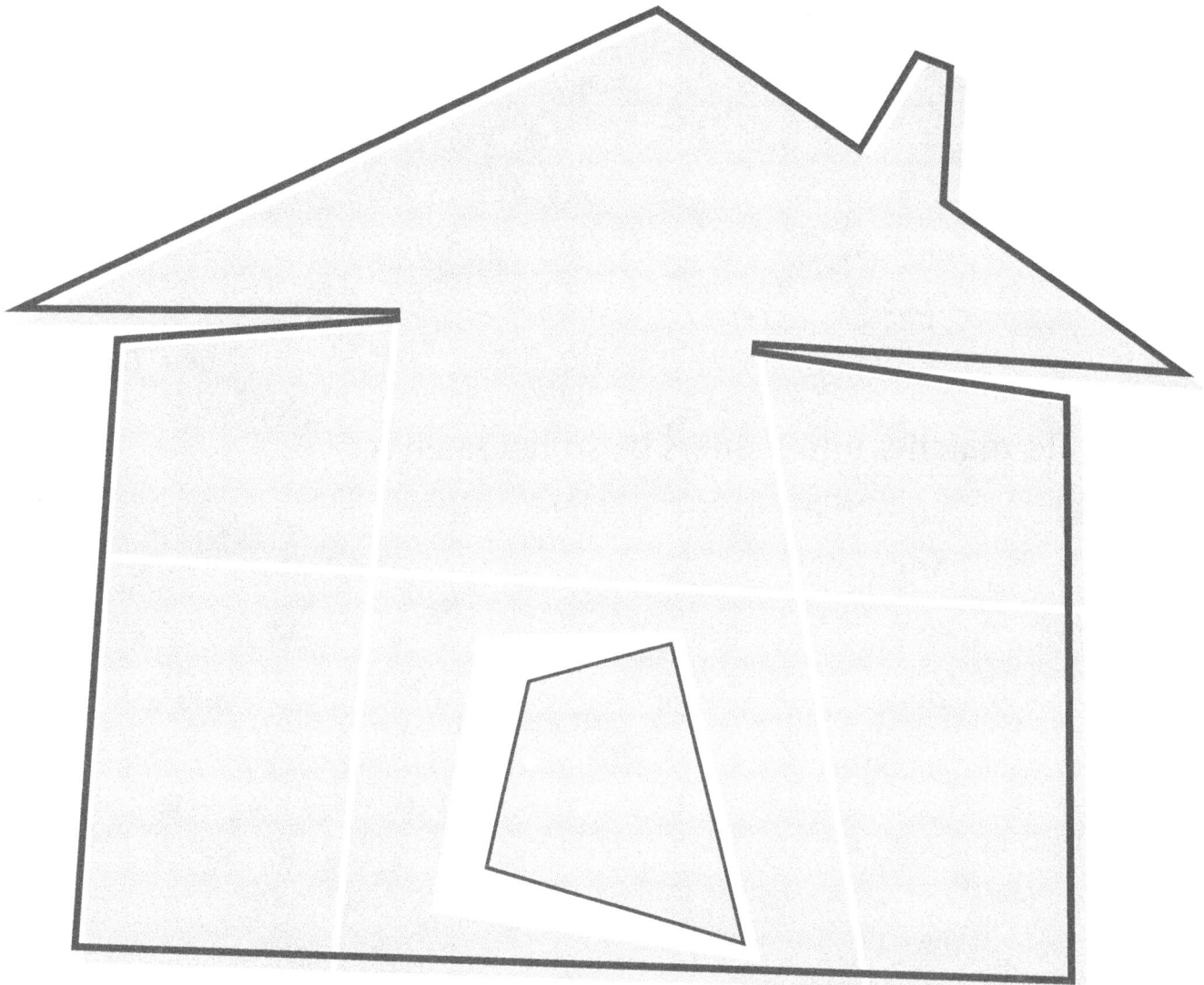

Stickers and Rewards: What I Can Earn at Home

With your caregiver, decide on the rewards that you will be able to earn at home for your efforts.

Rewards I can earn for completing the home practice activities at home:

 Reward #1

 Reward #2

 Reward #3

 Reward #4

 Reward #5

 Reward #6

Home Practice Checklist

1. Talk to other family members about fire-safety practices.

Check and date completed: _____

2. Help your caregiver post the Home Fire-Safety Search worksheet.

Check and date completed: _____

3. Search the home with your caregiver for matches, lighters or other fire-related materials. Remember, don't touch them yourself!

Check and date completed: _____

4. Plan a reward system with your caregiver for your fire safety efforts.

Check and date completed: _____

Session **1**

TAPP-C
Progress Note

Child

Fire Safety Begins at Home: Defining and Rewarding Fire-Safe Behaviour

Name: _____ File no.: _____ Session date: _____

Action plan:

☐ Client cancelled (specify action plan)   _____

☐ No show (specify action plan)   _____

☐ Clinician cancelled (specify action plan)   _____

☐ Attended Session 1 of the TAPP-C program

Fire involvement since last session?   ☐ Yes   ☐ No

Fire-safety education: ☐ In progress   ☐ Done   ☐ Not started   ☐ N/A

This session covered the following:

Covered	*Not covered*	
☐	☐	Began with joint meeting/check-in with child and caregiver
☐	☐	Reviewed goals and importance of the TAPP-C program
☐	☐	Helped the child to develop an understanding of why it is important to address fire involvement
☐	☐	Engaged the child as a collaborator in home fire safety; got the child on board to support the caregivers' efforts to establish control over ignition materials in the home
☐	☐	Built skills on how to search the home for ignition sources
☐	☐	Ended with joint meeting with child and caregiver
☐	☐	Discussed home practice activities

Outcome of session:

☐ Next session scheduled for: _____

☐ Treatment terminated (client initiated)   ☐ Treatment terminated (clinician initiated)

Additional notes:

_____   _____
Signature/Credentials   Date

Copyright © 2004 • Centre for Addiction and Mental Health • Office of the Fire Marshal of Ontario

Session 1 • Child **119**

Fire Safety Continues at Home: Monitoring Access to Ignition Materials and Learning SNAP™

Session at a glance

Background

Because children will inevitably find themselves in situations that put them at risk for fire involvement, the primary focus of this session is to help the child develop skills to assist him or her in refraining from touching fire-related materials.

Specifically, the child will learn Stop Now And Plan (SNAP™)[2]. SNAP™ is a cognitive behavioural strategy designed to assist children to exercise self-control and problem-solve. SNAP™ will be practised both in the session and at home.

The caregiver's session will focus on additional steps to monitor ignition sources within the home environment. Strategies for controlling access to smoking materials and for ensuring that the child is not bringing new ignition materials into the home are reviewed. As such, enlisting the child's co-operation with any additional steps that may be taken by the caregiver to restrict access to fire materials in the home is also an important goal of the present session.

---

[2] This manual contains trademarked materials under license granted by Earlscourt Child and Family Centre.

Goals

· Check in with the child and caregiver.

· Review the home practice activities with the child and the caregiver.

· Get the child on board with the idea that extra steps may be needed to make sure that ignition sources do not enter the home.

· Enlist the child's assistance in checking that everyone is following the rules about where to keep matches, lighters and other ignition sources and/or accelerants in the home.

· Emphasize the connection between using fire-safe behaviours and being rewarded.

· Learn to use SNAP™ (Stop Now And Plan).

· Wrap up with a joint meeting with the child and the caregiver.

If short of time

Your main goals are to review the Session 1 home practice and to begin to familiarize the child with SNAP™.

Materials needed

· blank white paper

· pencils

· coloured markers, crayons or pencil crayons

· Session 2 practice worksheets (p. 137)

· stickers or other incentives

· Session 2 progress note (p. 145)

Joint meeting with child and caregiver

Guidelines: 15 minutes

Clinician Note

The limits of confidentiality should be reviewed.

Check-in

> **Have there been any further episodes of fire involvement since the last appointment?**

If no further fire involvement is reported by the child or caregiver (and no evidence of covert play has been found by the caregiver), assume the best and praise both participants for their efforts and good work.

If further fire involvement has occurred, model for the child and caregiver an appropriate response that includes recognizing the seriousness of this behaviour and the need for problem-solving to determine what went wrong, as well as how to intervene further. (See Clinician Note.)

Clinician Note

An incident of fire-related relapse provides a good opportunity for the clinician to model an appropriate response that includes problem-solving what went wrong, establishing appropriate and meaningful consequences, and further tailoring the intervention to meet the family's needs.

Obtain specific details from the child as to the circumstances surrounding the fire-related incident. For instance, the child could be asked the following questions:

What ignition source was used? Where was the ignition source obtained? Where did the incident take place? Was anyone else involved? What was the child thinking and feeling just prior to the incident? How long has the child been thinking of doing this? What could have prevented the fire-related incident (from the child's point of view)?

- Introduce to the caregiver the notion of separating "education" from "consequences." While it is important that the child recognize the seriousness of this behaviour, now is probably not the best time for the clinician or caregiver to get into a lengthy review about the dangers of fire. The clinician can note that children and teens are likely to feel strong emotions during this time, such as anger at being caught or anxiety about how the incident will be dealt with. Therefore, highlight to caregivers that this is not an optimal time for learning. For instance, the clinician can let the child know that his or her actions were dangerous, but that further discussion of the incident will be saved for tomorrow. (As part of their home practice, ask the child and caregiver to further process the incident at home the following day. For instance, how much has the child retained from the first two sessions? Can he or she discuss how this particular incident was dangerous? What were the potential consequences?) Remind the participants that developing a proactive plan and appropriate consequences for dealing with any further fire involvement is part of the TAPP-C program and will be covered in detail in Session 4.

- Nevertheless, given that the child has been reinvolved with fire, now is an opportune time to have a preliminary discussion about consequences.

- What consequences could be given? (e.g., What privilege could be withdrawn, and for how long?) Ask the caregiver to anticipate any problem that may arise with the consequence given, and problem-solve potential strategies for dealing with the obstacle(s). If the clinician has time, he or she can offer to call at a designated time during the week to ensure that the consequences are followed through as planned. At the very least, make it clear that the consequences will be discussed during the following session.

Importantly, the information obtained about this fire-related incident will help the clinician to target further intervention, which can be built into today's session and/or home practice. For instance, if the child accessed a lighter from the kitchen cupboard, further problem-solving should occur regarding how to prevent access within the home.

Ask the following question:

What is your family's status and progress with the Fire Services Education portion of TAPP-C?

Review of home practice

Review the home practice activities from the previous session.

- Did the family carry out the initial home search activities?
- Are ignition sources and accelerants being stored in the appropriate manner?
- Did the family use the *Home Fire-Safety Search* worksheet, p. 22, and the *Home Practice Checklist,* p. 118, to monitor these activities?
- Was the child given a reward for fire-safe behaviours?

If the family was able to carry out these home fire-safety activities, be sure to use praise liberally for effort, rather than for success.

Be specific with your praise; for example, "It sounds like you did an excellent job searching all the rooms in your house," or "You made an excellent choice not touching the matches you saw on the table."

- Which aspects, if any, of the fire-safety activities did the child and caregiver find most helpful?

If problems arose, work with the child and the caregiver to (1) understand the obstacles to carrying out the tasks, and (2) amend the home practice activity so as to maximize their chances for success.

Once the barriers to completing a home practice activity are clarified, the clinician, caregiver and child can problem-solve to determine how the goal can be accomplished. For example, the child and/or caregiver may first need to break down the new tasks, tackling component parts of the task separately rather than as a whole. Once the home practice activity has been modified, and perhaps rehearsed in the session, the task can be reassigned for next session.

Keep in mind that it is optimal to add intervention sessions until the child and caregiver have had an opportunity to experience at least partial success in each of their home practice activities.

Clinician Note

The child and caregiver need to buy into the importance of stopping the fire involvement and to have accepted responsibility for preventing further fire involvement before moving on to the rest of the contents of Session 2.

For additional information, please see the Special Issues section on the Reluctant or Resistant Caregiver, p. 203.

Child alone

Get the child on board with the idea that extra steps may be needed to make sure that ignition sources do not enter the home.

Guidelines: 15 minutes

The child should understand that all family members, including the child and caregiver, will be following rules about ignition sources in the home. For example, caregivers who are smokers should not carry more than one lighter, and will need to check before entering the home that they are not carrying any additional ignition materials with them.

If the child is suspected of bringing matches or lighters into the home (or if the child has done so in the past), keeping the home and child safe from fire may necessitate rules about searching the child's pockets and belongings when entering the home. These search rules should be framed as a safety issue and will be negotiated with the child's caregiver (e.g., some children are more comfortable turning their own pockets inside out for "inspection" rather than being physically searched by the caregiver).

Many children will initially respond to this idea with the refrain that the caregiver does not trust them, but they are more accepting of this policy when the clinician emphasizes that it is to keep the child safe and out of trouble. Indeed, an important role played by the clinician in every session with the child is to prepare the child for new family rules and expectations and to enlist the child's co-operation with these changes as much as is possible.

Use the following questions to complete the Keeping Ignition Materials and Accelerants under Caregiver Control *worksheet. (Even if this topic is not applicable now, the concept of checking the child's person and/or belongings should at least be introduced as something that could possibly be a necessary practice in the future.)*

- **How do matches and lighters come into your home?**
- **How many times have you brought matches and lighters into your home?**
- **How could your family ensure that you do not bring matches or lighters into your home?**
- **Who needs to be included in the plan and what do they need to do to help?**
- **What role can you play in making sure that new matches and lighters do not come into the home?**

If appropriate, discuss what can be done to reduce access to ignition materials for a youth who smokes.

Children or adolescent smokers with a history of fire involvement present unique challenges. These youth should be prohibited from carrying matches or lighters on their person. Note that the Court almost always imposes this type of restriction for any youth convicted of a fire-related offence. Indeed, court-ordered sanctions for firesetting sometimes include prohibitions against the possession of any incendiary device, including a lit cigarette.

For more information, please see the section on Adolescents in the Special Issues section, p. 207.

If the caregiver or youth is motivated to stop smoking or is contemplating it, you should reinforce the idea and begin to problem-solve the steps toward achieving this goal. Part of this includes providing information; for example, on smoking cessation programs in the local community. Discuss the level of involvement that the youth or caregiver could expect from you, even if you are only "checking in" on her or his progress.

Unfortunately, it has been our experience that older youth or caregivers are rarely willing to consider giving up smoking. If the youth is going to continue to smoke, then a plan should be negotiated with the youth and caregiver about where he or she is permitted to smoke and about how he or she is going to obtain a light to smoke.

Many adolescents who set a fire or use fire inappropriately do not do so in a malicious or planned way. Rather, many of these youth tend to be impulsive and have a history of playing with their lighters or matches in their pockets or purses in a more habitual or mindless way. They use their lighter or matches without thinking—because they have immediate access to these ignition sources in their pockets or purses.

A very effective way to prevent adolescents from using lighters or matches impulsively is to restrict them from carrying these items. When the adolescent does want to smoke, he or she will have to seek out a lighter (and possibly adult supervision). The delay that becomes necessary to accomplish this will, in and of itself, help prevent impulsive or unplanned fire involvement.

Many adolescents are aware, or can be made aware, of the impulsive or habitual nature of their lighter play. They often agree to not carry lighters or matches as a way of preventing impulsive use of fire when the strategy and its rationale are explained to them and concerns about their safety or criminal liability are highlighted.

Use the following questions to help the adolescent think about rules for smoking and possibly for other family members or visitors who smoke:

How often do you smoke?

Are there rules about your smoking? For example, where and when are you permitted to smoke?

- Why should there be rules about smoking?

- How would such rules be helpful?

- Should there be rules about your access to smoking materials?

- What would the goals of these rules be?

- What about other smokers in your home; should there also be rules for these individuals?

- What message might such rules convey?

Enlist the child's assistance in checking that everyone is following the rules about where to keep matches, lighters or other ignition sources in the home.

Guidelines: 15 minutes

Checking that everyone is following the rules regarding where to keep matches and lighters should be a regular family routine and one that includes all family members, especially the child with fire involvement. Everyone needs to understand that this is a routine to keep the family and the identified child safe from fire.

Families participating in the TAPP-C intervention have been very successful in stopping the child's fire involvement. Nevertheless, some children who have successfully stopped their fire involvement for some period of time do start again. Our follow-up data suggest that there is a link between recidivism and families who stopped using the fire-safety practices because they believed that the child had lost interest in fire.

Remind the child that the steps the caregiver is taking to control or limit access to ignition materials are the new fire-safe behaviours that are replacing the old fire-dangerous behaviours of the family. As such, most of these behaviours or routines should continue indefinitely.

Ideally, some of the more intrusive measures, like those that involve searching the child's belongings on return home from the community, can be stopped eventually as the child becomes free from fire involvement over a prolonged time interval.

Use the following questions to initiate a discussion about monitoring ignition sources in the home. Review questions 2 and 3 of the previously completed Home Fire-Safety Search *worksheet, p. 22.*

- Once everyone knows what they need to do to keep matches and lighters and other ignition sources secure, how can your family check that everyone is following the family rules about where to keep matches and lighters?

- Would a regular checking of the home to make sure that matches or lighters are not left unattended or in places that are accessible be helpful?
- How could you be of help in conducting these checks or searches?
- How could your family remember to do these searches?

Emphasize the connection between using fire-safe behaviours and being rewarded.

Guidelines: 10 minutes

Review question 4 of the previously completed *Home Fire-Safety Search* caregiver worksheet, p. 22.

Remind the child that TAPP-C stresses the importance of rewarding efforts at fire safety. The child may enjoy generating reward ideas; these ideas can be revisited during the joint meeting with the caregiver at the end of the session.

Clinician Note

In this session, one reward that is discussed is for effort around the checking or monitoring that fire-starting materials are kept as agreed.

It is not good practice to make the reward contingent on the child not finding matches or lighters. This may only encourage the child to become more lax with the searches or more devious about hiding fire-starting materials.

Session 4 will focus on effective consequences and how the caregiver should respond if the child is found with matches or lighters or involved in another episode of fire involvement.

Introduce SNAP™ (Stop Now And Plan).

Guidelines: 20 minutes

This portion of the session aims to introduce preliminary cognitive behavioural skills that the child can use to stop him- or herself from touching or playing with ignition materials. The core skills for controlling impulsive and/or antisocial behaviours are the same whether the impulse is to steal, hit someone or light a fire.

The SNAP™ program was developed by the Earlscourt Child and Family Centre (ECFC). SNAP™ has embedded core cognitive behavioural skills into a format that is concrete and easy for children and their caregivers to use.

The TAPP-C program uses fire-specific vignettes and examples within the SNAP™ format to teach children impulse control with regard to fire involvement. However, because fire involvement can be episodic and/or occur infrequently, SNAP™ can also be learned and practised using other problem situations or behaviours relevant to the child. For very young children and adolescents, this intervention will need to be modified to ensure that it is developmentally appropriate and relevant. (See the Special Issues sections on Adolescents, p. 207, and Preschoolers, p. 206.)

Use the following questions to engage the child's interest:

- **Do kids ever do things without thinking? What kinds of things have you done without thinking?**

- **Do kids ever get into trouble because they react too fast?**

- **Do kids ever get hurt because they do something without thinking?**

- **Do kids sometimes play with fire without thinking about what could happen?**

Here are some further ideas for discussion:

All children and adolescents sometimes do things without thinking. They react too fast and do things that could get them into trouble or could cause them to hurt themselves or someone else.

Playing with fire is one of the things that can hurt someone or get you into trouble.

In this session, we are going to learn something children can do to help stop them from playing with fire. Listen carefully to the following scenario.

Role-play the following scenario and use the following questions to guide the child's thinking and problem-solving.

Scenario

"Hmm, my mother left her lighter on the counter and I really want to touch it and try it out. She is on the phone so she'll never find out that I touched it. I'll just light it one or two times and put it back. It's really exciting and a bit scary to use a lighter."

- **What is the problem facing the child in this story? (He wants to try his mother's lighter.)**

- What kinds of thoughts are going through his head? ("I want to try that lighter." "It won't hurt anyone.")

- How does the child feel? (excited, scared)

- What is the first thing the child should do? (Use SNAP™—Stop Now And Plan.)

- How can he *stop* himself from touching the lighter? (He could put his hands in his pocket or take a deep breath.)

- What would be a good *plan?* (one that will keep him from touching the lighter)

Demonstrate using SNAP™ by continuing the scenario.

"Hmm, my mother left her lighter on the counter and I really, really want to try it. I wonder how that paper napkin would burn? I'll try lighting it quickly in the sink and she will never find out. This will be really fun."

SNAP your fingers, take a step back, put your hands in your pockets, take a deep breath and continue the scenario.

"Whoa, I shouldn't do that, I am not allowed to touch a lighter. If I do, I could get into big trouble. I might even start a fire. But I really want to try it … *stop,* Count to 10. … *think,* what am I going to do? Okay, I need a *plan.* I know. I am going to find my mom and tell her that she left her lighter out. That way no one will get hurt and I won't get in trouble."

Ask the following questions about the scenario:

- 1. How did I *stop* myself from touching the lighter?

- 2. What kind of things did I do?

- 3. What did I do next?

- 4. What kind of *plan* did I make?

Help the child learn the SNAP™ skill steps.

Stop myself. (Use the *SNAP™ Wheel of Self-Control and Wheel of Plans* worksheet.)

> *Ask the child:*
>
> **When you are feeling like you want to touch or take matches or start a fire (fill in the appropriate phrase), what is the first thing you need to do? (Use SNAP™.)**

Complete the *Stop* portion of the "Wheel of Self-Control." Have the child generate ideas about how to *stop* him- or herself. For example, the child could:

· take a deep breath

· count to ten and/or

· put hands in pocket.

These are strategies that a person can use to calm the physiological symptoms associated with emotional arousal such as the excitement at finding a lighter or the thought of seeing fire.

> *Ask the child the following questions:*
>
> **Can you tell me about some times that you (or someone else) had to stop yourself from doing something you shouldn't?**
>
> **Would the ideas for things to do on the *Stop* wheel have helped you?**
>
> **Which things work best for you?**

Make a plan. (Use the *SNAP™ Wheel of Self-Control and Wheel of Plans* worksheet.)

> *Ask the child:*
>
> **After you have stopped yourself from touching or taking the matches (fill in the appropriate phrase), what is the next thing you should do? (Make a plan.)**

Complete the Plan section of the Wheel of Self-Control. Have the child generate a plan for behaviours that he or she can do instead of touching the matches.

For example, the child could:

· tell an adult

· ask for help

· distract him- or herself or

· walk away.

A key to executing a successful plan is for the child to able to use effective calming strategies and then positive self-talk to get to the next step.

Conduct in-session practice/role-plays of SNAP™.

Use the *SNAP™ In-Session Practice* worksheet. Based on what you know about the child (antecedents and pattern of fire involvement), set up hypothetical vignettes in the session to practise skill-building with the child through role-playing. For example, has the child been tempted when angry or bored or because of peer pressure? Set the scenario up accordingly. For example, Tammy goes to the park and her friend is there with a lighter doing fancy lighter tricks. She suggests Tammy try to do a lighter trick.

This session should introduce all of the steps to SNAP™. However, the primary emphasis should be on helping the child learn strategies for stopping him- or herself from touching an ignition source. Stopping is the first step in SNAP™.

The plan component and the evaluation of consequences will be covered and practised in the next two sessions. Nevertheless, older children may move through all steps more quickly and benefit from practising the sequence in its entirety. As such, the clinician should be familiar with these next components.

If available, use a video camera to record the role-plays and for review and feedback about the steps.

The clinician should first role-play a likely scenario while the child observes. Based on the role-play, have the child describe the problem and the strategies used to calm down or not touch the ignition source, and then have the child describe the plan.

Ask the child for suggestions about how it could have been done differently or better by the clinician. Redo the scenario incorporating the child's feedback.

Next, the child should practise a role-play while the clinician videotapes/observes it. Replay the video and give feedback. Have the child redo the scenario taking the feedback into account.

Remind the child to talk out loud, so that he or she can generate solutions to the problem. For at least one of the role-plays, it will be important to practise skills using a hypothetical vignette in which the child is faced with finding matches or lighters in the home or in the community.

Remind the child that SNAP™ can be used with other behaviours that get a person into trouble as well.[3] If there is time, have the child choose another likely scenario and carry out the SNAP™ steps with your help.

The child should be provided with a great deal of encouragement and praise for his or her ideas and participation.

Wrap-up and joint meeting with child and caregiver

Guidelines: 15 minutes

Provide a brief review of the content of the session and the Home Fire-Safety Search. Focus on the co-operation and efforts of the child and caregiver and provide liberal praise and recognition for these efforts.

Have the child show the caregiver his or her use of SNAP™.

Assist the child with SNAP™ (as required) to model such assistance for the caregiver.

Use the *Keeping Ignition Materials and Accelerants under Caregiver Control* worksheet to help the child and/or the caregiver practise telling other family members who were not present at the session about any additional rules for matches and lighters, etc. This is also an excellent venue for getting the child on board with these new rules.

Have the child and caregiver practise a pocket and/or bag search together, if it will be required in the home.

---

[3] For more information see *SNAP™ Children's Group Manual* and *SNAP™: A Parenting Guide*. For more information, see www.earlscourt.on.ca.

Discuss home practice.

The following are the suggested home practice activities to be completed before the next session:

1. The caregiver will post the updated *Home Fire-Safety Search* worksheet, p. 22.

2. The caregiver and the child should schedule two occasions when together they will check that matches, lighters and other ignition materials are being stored as planned.

3. The caregiver will help the child practise SNAP™ in actual problematic situations that occur for the child. However, if such occasions do not occur naturally, the caregiver will schedule two times before the next session to help the child practise (e.g., role-play) SNAP™. The caregiver will also help the child complete two *SNAP™ Tracking Sheets*.

4. The caregiver should reward the family for checking to insure that ignition sources and/or accelerants in the home are secure and that new ignition sources and/or accelerants have not come into the home. The caregiver should reward the child or youth for practising SNAP™.

5. The caregiver and the child together should use the *Home Fire-Safety Search* worksheet and the *Home Practice Checklist* to record what has been completed of the home practice activities.

Fire Safety Continues at Home: Monitoring Access to Ignition Materials and Learning SNAP™

Date: _____

Keeping Ignition Materials and Accelerants under Caregiver Control

Rules for keeping ignition materials and accelerants under caregiver control:

1. *e.g., Johnny will empty his pockets and school bag when coming into the house.*

2. *e.g., Dad will check his pockets for lighters when coming home from work.*

3. *e.g., Visitors to the home will be reminded to carry their lighters with them.*

SNAP™
Wheel of Self-Control
and
Wheel of Plans

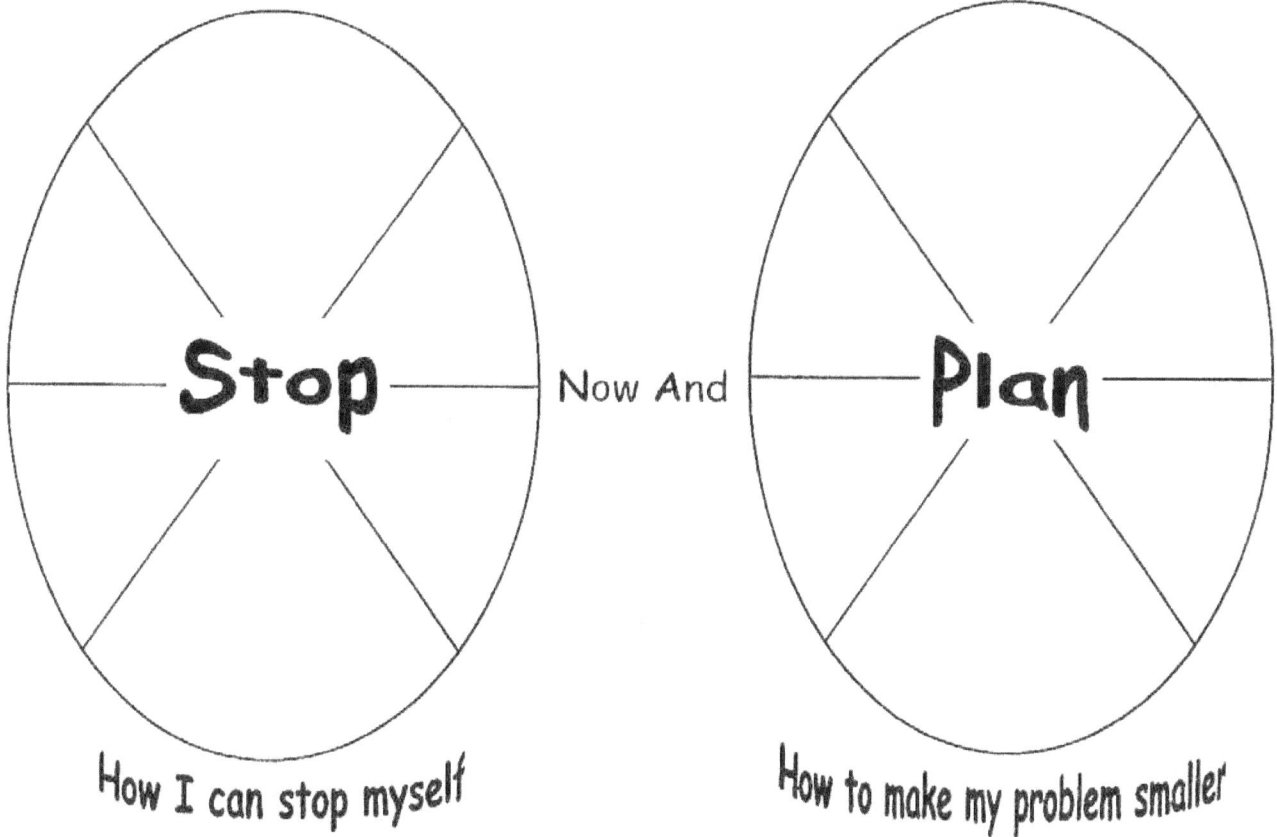

Stop ——— Now And ——— Plan

How I can stop myself

How to make my problem smaller

SNAP™ In-Session Practice

Date: _____

Scenario:

_____

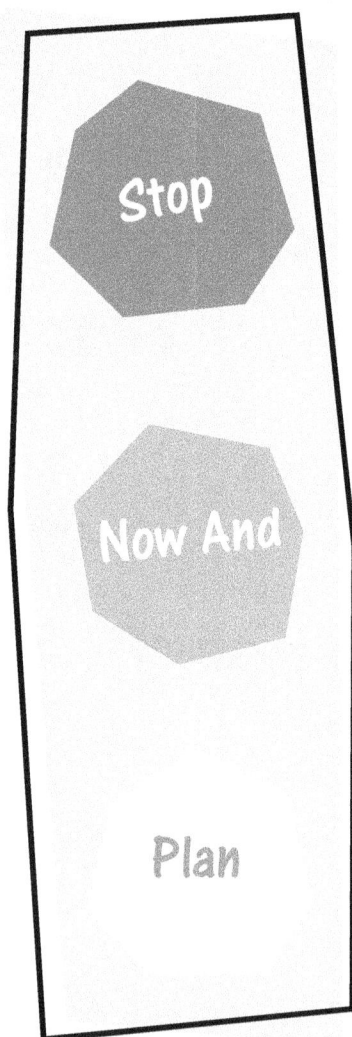

1. Ways I can stop myself (fill out the wheel of self-control)

_____

_____

_____

2. Thoughts that will help

_____

_____

_____

3. Things I can do instead (fill out the wheel of plans)

_____

_____

_____

SNAP™ Tracking Sheet

Name: _____ Date: _____

What time of day was it? ☐ Morning ☐ Afternoon ☐ Evening ☐ Nighttime

Where was I? ☐ Home ☐ School ☐ Community

Who was I with? ☐ Alone ☐ Friends ☐ Brother/Sister ☐ Caregiver

What happened? _____

How was I feeling? _____

What was I thinking? _____

Ways I stopped myself...

1 _____ 2 _____ 3 _____

Thoughts that helped...

1 _____ 2 _____ 3 _____

My plan was...

1 _____ 2 _____ 3 _____

How did I do?

I made my problem...   ☐ Smaller   ☐ Same   ☐ Bigger

My caregiver's signature: _____

SNAP™ Tracking Sheet

Name: _____ Date: _____

What time of day was it? ☐ Morning ☐ Afternoon ☐ Evening ☐ Nighttime

Where was I? ☐ Home ☐ School ☐ Community

Who was I with? ☐ Alone ☐ Friends ☐ Brother/Sister ☐ Caregiver

What happened? _____

How was I feeling? _____

What was I thinking? _____

Ways I stopped myself…

1 _____ 2 _____ 3 _____

Thoughts that helped…

1 _____ 2 _____ 3 _____

My plan was…

1 _____ 2 _____ 3 _____

How did I do?

I made my problem…   ☐ Smaller   ☐ Same   ☐ Bigger

My caregiver's signature: _____

Home Practice Checklist

1. Help your caregiver post the updated Home Fire-Safety Search worksheet.

> Check and date completed: _____

2. Help your caregiver check that matches and lighters are being kept as planned before the next session (twice).

> Check and date completed: _____

> Check and date completed: _____

3. Practise SNAP™ (twice).

> Check and date completed: _____

> Check and date completed: _____

4. Plan a reward system with your caregiver for your fire-safety efforts.

> Check and date completed: _____

Fire Safety Continues at Home: Monitoring Access to Ignition Materials and Learning SNAP™

Name: _____   File no.: _____   Session date: _____

Action plan:

☐ Client cancelled (specify action plan)   _____

☐ No show (specify action plan)   _____

☐ Clinician cancelled (specify action plan)   _____

☐ Attended Session 2 of the TAPP-C program

Fire involvement since last session?   ☐ Yes   ☐ No

Fire-safety education: ☐ In progress   ☐ Done   ☐ Not started   ☐ N/A

This session covered the following:

Covered	*Not covered*	
☐	☐	Began with joint meeting/check-in with child and caregiver
☐	☐	Reviewed previous home practice
☐	☐	Got the child on board with the idea that extra steps may be necessary to make sure that ignition sources do not enter the home
☐	☐	Enlisted the child's assistance in checking that everyone is following the rules about where to keep matches, lighters or other ignition sources in the home
☐	☐	Emphasized the connection between using fire-safe behaviours and being rewarded
☐	☐	Introduced SNAP™
☐	☐	Helped child learn SNAP™ steps (Focus on STOP.)
☐	☐	Ended with joint meeting with child and caregiver
☐	☐	Discussed home practice activities

Outcome of session:

☐ Next session scheduled for: _____

☐ Treatment terminated (client initiated)   ☐ Treatment terminated (clinician initiated)

Additional notes:

_____   _____
Signature/Credentials   Date

Session

3

Child

Fire Safety Away from Home: Preventing Situations that Lead to Fire Involvement

Session at a glance

Background

Sessions 1 and 2 targeted family teamwork with regard to rules, access prevention and monitoring of ignition sources. This session focuses on identifying common antecedents to fire involvement and developing and practising coping skills to increase fire-safe behaviours and decrease the risk of fire-dangerous behaviours.

Both intrapersonal and environmental risk factors have been found to be associated with fire involvement. Among the most common intrapersonal factors for a child's fire involvement are the following:

· impulsivity (poor self-control and problem-solving)

· boredom and

· curiosity about fire.

Sometimes negative emotions, such as anger, frustration or anxiety, are also precursors to acting-out behaviours, such as firesetting.

Common environmental antecedents to fire involvement include:

· the absence of adult supervision

· the absence of structured activities and

· the presence of antisocial peers.

This session will help educate the child about situations that put the child at risk for fire involvement, and how the child can assist the caregiver to prevent such situations.

However, the primary focus of the session is on continuing to practise using SNAP™ to assist the child to not touch fire-related materials.

In this session, the child will use SNAP™ to identify thoughts that may promote fire involvement (thinking mistakes) and to substitute thoughts that would help the child avoid touching ignition materials. For children who are presenting with fire involvement as one of many difficulties, please refer to the Special Issues section on Comorbid Conditions, p. 206.

The caregiver session emphasizes strategies for insuring fire safety when the child is away from the caregiver. Specifically, the session will help caregivers to take a proactive stance in planning for the child's time outside of caregiver supervision. Common antecedents of fire involvement will be identified and the caregiver will develop and practise skills related to informing others about the child's needs, monitoring the child's whereabouts, activity planning, and increasing the child's opportunity to interact with prosocial peers.

Goals

· Check in with the child and caregiver.

· Review home practice activity with the child and caregiver.

· Review common antecedents to fire involvement.

· Get the child to co-operate with the caregiver in monitoring the whereabouts of the child.

· Practise more with SNAP™—identifying thinking errors and thoughts that help.

· Wrap up and discuss the home practice activities with the caregiver and the child.

If short of time

Your main goal is to focus on a specific component of SNAP™: helping the child to identify and practise "thoughts that help" in stopping fire involvement.

Materials needed

· blank white paper

· pencils

· coloured markers, crayons or pencil crayons

· Session 3 practice worksheets (p. 157)

· stickers or other incentives

· Session 3 progress note (p. 167)

Joint meeting with child and caregiver

Guidelines: 15 minutes

Clinician Note

The limits of confidentiality should be reviewed.

Check-in

▪ **Have there been any further episodes of fire involvement since the last appointment?**

If no further fire involvement has been reported by the child or caregiver, assume the best and praise both participants for their efforts and good work.

If further fire involvement has occurred, model for the child and caregiver an appropriate response that includes recognizing the seriousness of this behaviour and the need for problem-solving to determine what went wrong, as well as how to intervene further. (For further details, see Session 2.)

An incident of fire-related relapse provides a good opportunity for in-session review and further learning about:

· prevention of situations that lead to fire involvement

· the importance of controlling access to ignition materials and accelerants and

· practising with SNAP™.

If appropriate, ask the following question:

▪ **What is your family's status and progress with regard to the Fire Services Education portion of TAPP-C?**

Review of home practice

Review the home practice activities from the previous session.

· Did the caregiver and child discuss any additional rules about ignition sources and accelerants or home checks with other family members or caregivers?

· Did the family carry out the home-checking activities?

· Are ignition sources being stored in the appropriate manner?

· Did the child practise using SNAP™?

· Was the child rewarded for her or his efforts?

· Did the family use the *Home Fire-Safety Search* worksheet, p. 22, and the child *Home Practice Checklist,* p. 143, to monitor these activities?

· Was the child given a reward for fire-safe behaviours?

If the family was able to carry out some of the home fire-safety activities, be sure to use praise liberally for effort, rather than for success. Be specific with your praise. Which aspects (if any) of the fire-safety proofing did they find most helpful?

If problems arose, work with the child and caregiver to (1) understand the obstacles to carrying out the tasks, and (2) amend the home practice activity so as to maximize their chances for success.

Child alone

Help the child identify common antecedents to fire involvement and determine what can be done about them.

Guidelines: 15 minutes

Use the following questions to begin a discussion with the child about common antecedents to fire involvement. While tailoring the discussion to the child's needs, the child should finish this part of the session with some awareness that lack of supervision, lack of planned activities, and/or the presence of antisocial peers are common precursors to a child's fire-dangerous behaviours.

Where has past fire involvement taken place?

What were you doing?

Who were you with?

Where was your caregiver?

Use the following questions to engage the child as a collaborator in possible solutions:

■ **What kinds of things might help keep these situations from occurring in the future?**

■ **What could your caregiver do that might help?**

■ **What could you do that might help?**

Show the child the *Times without Supervision* worksheet and explain it briefly. Let the child know that although every child is different, there appear to be common situations that lead to fire involvement.

· It is almost always the case that a caregiver is not around at the time.

· It also seems to be the case that the child is often just "hanging out," not doing anything that was planned or productive.

· Sometimes the child is with other kids who get into trouble.

Explain that these are the kinds of situations the caregiver will be learning to prevent.

As with the previous family fire-safety practices, getting the child to comply and assist with new routines and expectations will be critical to his or her success. Ask the following questions:

■ **How do you think the *Times without Supervision* worksheet might help?**

■ **What could your role be?**

Next, have the child complete the *Triggers to Fire Involvement* worksheet. Not only will this worksheet help identify places, activities and people that lead to trouble, the worksheet should also generate discussion about situations that help children stay out of trouble (e.g., fire involvement).

Let the child know that the caregiver will be asking questions about the child's whereabouts to make sure that the child is safe, and will try and enlist the child's co-operation with these efforts to keep him or her safe. For example, help the child complete answers to the following questions:

■ **Where can you play that you are safe?**

■ **What kinds of activities keep you busy and out of trouble?**

■ **Which friends do you have that are least likely to get you into trouble?**

Identify thoughts that promote fire involvement (thinking mistakes), and substitute thoughts that help.

Guidelines: 15 minutes

Ask the child for a likely scenario that includes peers and fire involvement. For example, use the scenario and the questions that follow to guide the child's thinking and problem-solving and to stimulate discussion.

SCENARIO

"My best friend brought a lighter to school and he wants me to try it."

OR

"My friends were hanging around outside the coffee shop throwing lit matches into the garbage container, and they threw me the pack of matches."

- **What is the problem facing the child in this scenario?**

- **What is the first thing the child needs to do? (Use SNAP™.)**

- **What kinds of things can the child do to stop his involvement?**

- **What kinds of thoughts are going through the child's head when he thinks about the lighter?**

- **Will some of these thoughts make the child think that it's okay to touch the lighter?**

- **Will some of these thoughts make the child realize it is not okay to touch the lighter?**

Use the *Thinking Mistakes versus Thoughts that Help* worksheet to help the child make a list of thoughts that might lead him or her to think that it is okay to touch an ignition source.

Some sample thoughts might be the following:

- **It will burn really cool.**
- **I'm just going to try it; I'm not going to burn anything.**
- **I'm not going to hurt myself just trying it once.**
- **My friend thinks it's okay, so it must be.**
- **My friend is not afraid of a lighter.**
- **My friend will think I'm a goof if I don't try it.**
- **I won't get caught, so it's okay.**

Go through each thought on the child's list, and ask the child to say whether this thought would tell the child it's okay or not okay to touch the ignition source.

Using the list, the clinician may say, "So, some thoughts really do make kids think it's okay to touch a lighter. Let's think of some other, opposite thoughts or ones that would tell the child it's *not okay* to touch the lighter":

EXAMPLES OF THINKING MISTAKES	EXAMPLES OF THOUGHTS THAT HELP
The lighter will burn really cool.	The flame may burn me.
I'm not going to burn anything.	I could start a fire even if I don't want to.
My friend thinks it's okay.	It's never okay to play with a lighter.
My friend is not afraid.	My friend should know it's dangerous.
My friend will think I'm a goof.	Doing what's safe is more important.
I won't get caught, so it's okay.	I better not because I'm gonna get caught.
	Even if I don't get caught, it's not okay.

Once the child has had the opportunity to become familiar with the idea of thinking mistakes or thoughts that might lead to believing it's okay to touch an ignition source, help the child learn the SNAP™ steps, incorporating and emphasizing thoughts that help into the sequence.

SCENARIO (CONTINUED)

"My best friend brought a lighter to school, and he really wants me to try it. The flame looks really cool; I'd really like to try it. I won't hurt anything. He's going to think I'm a goof if I don't."

Clinician SNAPS her fingers, takes a step back, puts her hands in her pocket and takes a deep breath. STOP. THINK.

"Whoa, I shouldn't do that; I am not allowed to touch a lighter. If I do, I could get into big trouble. I might even start a fire. I might burn myself. STOP. THINK. "What am I going to do? This is hard, but I know I can do it. I need a PLAN. I know: I am going to walk away and tell my friend that playing with a lighter is very dangerous and that someone could get hurt. That way I won't get in trouble."

Guide the child to identify the skill steps (self-control and problem-solving). Ask the following questions:

How did the child STOP himself from touching the lighter?

What did he do?

What kind of thoughts did he have that helped?

What is the next thing he needed to do? (PLAN)

What kind of PLAN did he make?

Was the plan a good one?

In-session practice (Use the *SNAP™ In-Session Practice* worksheet.)

Guidelines: 30 minutes

As in Session 2, help the child generate situations appropriate for him or her in which to practise SNAP™. The session should include all SNAP™ steps but, in this session, emphasize the role of thinking mistakes that lead the child to believe it is okay to play with fire versus coping thoughts that remind the child that playing with fire is risky and not okay. The PLAN component of SNAP™ and the evaluation of consequences will be emphasized in the next session.

If available, use a video camera to record the role-plays, and to review and get feedback about the steps. The clinician should first do the role-play and get the child to answer questions and provide feedback. The child should then be encouraged to role-play situations of relevance to the child, and the clinician should videotape it and provide feedback.

Remind the child that SNAP™ can also be used and practised in other problem situations.

Wrap-up and joint meeting with the child and caregiver

Guidelines: 15 minutes

Provide a brief review of the skills learned in the session. Focus on the efforts and progress of the child and caregiver in skill development, and provide liberal praise and recognition for these efforts.

Have the child show the caregiver the steps to SNAP™, and help the child teach the caregiver these steps. Have the child explain the thoughts that help.

Have the caregiver show the child the *Times without Supervision* worksheet and help the caregiver explain the principles involved.

Have the caregiver inform the child about the other caregivers who will be told about the family's fire-safety practices.

Discuss home practice.

The following are the suggested home practice activities to be completed before the next session:

1. The child and the caregiver should conduct the home check for ignition materials and update the previously completed *Home Fire-Safety Search* worksheet.

2. Once a day until the next session, the caregiver should sit with the child and plan for times that day or the following day that the child will be out of the caregiver's view or unsupervised. Together they should complete the *Times without Supervision* worksheet.

3. The caregiver should tell others who will be supervising the child about the fire involvement of the child and about the fire-safety routines that will help.

4. The caregiver should help the child practise SNAP™ and use thoughts that help. Complete two *SNAP™ Tracking Sheets*.

5. The caregiver should reward the child for fire-safe behaviours and for using SNAP™.

6. The caregiver and child should use the *Home Practice Checklist* to check off the tasks they have completed.

Optional activity

Using the *Safe Activities* worksheet, the caregiver should make a list with the child of activities that the child can do when unsupervised in the home or when the child is in the community on his or her own. Assign each activity a location and check-in time.

Fire Safety Away from Home: Preventing Situations that Lead to Fire Involvement

Date: _____

Times without Supervision

Answer the questions to help plan for times the child will be without supervision:

When will the child be
without supervision? _____

Where will
the child be? _____

What will the
child be doing? _____

Who will be
with the child? _____

Is access to ignition
materials a concern? _____

Check in time: When
should I check in with my child? _____

Things the caregiver can do
to keep the child safe: _____

Things the child can do that
would help keep him- or herself safe: _____

Triggers
to
Fire Involvement

Situation 1

Where am I? _____

What am I doing? _____

Who am I with? _____

How am I feeling? _____

Where is my caregiver? _____

Situation 2

Where am I? _____

What am I doing? _____

Who am I with? _____

How am I feeling? _____

Where is my caregiver? _____

Thinking Mistakes Versus Thoughts that Help

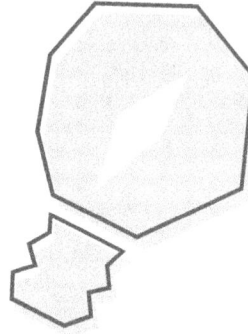

Thinking Mistakes!

1. _____

2. _____

3. _____

4. _____

5. _____

Thoughts that Help!

1. _____

2. _____

3. _____

4. _____

5. _____

SNAP™ In-Session Practice

Date: _____

Scenario:

_____

1. Ways I can stop myself (fill out the wheel of self-control)

_____

_____

_____

2. Thoughts that will help

_____

_____

_____

3. Things I can do instead (fill out the wheel of plans)

_____

_____

_____

SNAP™ Tracking Sheet

Name: _____ Date: _____

What time of day was it? ☐ Morning ☐ Afternoon ☐ Evening ☐ Nighttime

Where was I? ☐ Home ☐ School ☐ Community

Who was I with? ☐ Alone ☐ Friends ☐ Brother/Sister ☐ Caregiver

What happened? _____

How was I feeling? _____

What was I thinking? _____

Ways I stopped myself...

1 _____ 2 _____ 3 _____

Thoughts that helped...

1 _____ 2 _____ 3 _____

My plan was...

1 _____ 2 _____ 3 _____

How did I do?

I made my problem...   ☐ Smaller   ☐ Same   ☐ Bigger

My caregiver's signature: _____

SNAP™ Tracking Sheet

Name: _____ Date: _____

What time of day was it? ☐ Morning ☐ Afternoon ☐ Evening ☐ Nighttime

Where was I? ☐ Home ☐ School ☐ Community

Who was I with? ☐ Alone ☐ Friends ☐ Brother/Sister ☐ Caregiver

What happened? _____

How was I feeling? _____

What was I thinking? _____

Ways I stopped myself…

1 _____ 2 _____ 3 _____

Thoughts that helped…

1 _____ 2 _____ 3 _____

My plan was…

1 _____ 2 _____ 3 _____

How did I do?

I made my problem… ☐ Smaller ☐ Same ☐ Bigger

My caregiver's signature: _____

Home Practice Checklist

1. Help your caregiver post the updated Home Fire-Safety Search worksheet.

   Check and date completed: _____

2. Help your caregiver check that matches and lighters are being kept as planned before the next session (twice).

   Check and date completed: _____   Check and date completed: _____

3. Practise SNAP™ (twice).

   Check and date completed: _____   Check and date completed: _____

4. Plan for times without supervision.

   Check and date completed: _____   Check and date completed: _____

   Check and date completed: _____   Check and date completed: _____

   Check and date completed: _____   Check and date completed: _____

   Check and date completed: _____   Check and date completed: _____

5. Were you rewarded for your fire-safety efforts?

   Check and date completed: _____

Safe Activities

Things my child can do that are safe:

What	Where	For How Long
e.g., attend swimming lessons	e.g., community centre	e.g., 60 minutes

TAPP-C

Progress Note

Child

Fire Safety Away from Home: Preventing Situations that Lead to Fire Involvement

Name: _____   File no.: _____   Session date: _____

Action plan:

☐ Client cancelled (specify action plan)   _____

☐ No show (specify action plan)   _____

☐ Clinician cancelled (specify action plan)   _____

☐ Attended Session 3 of the TAPP-C program

Fire involvement since last session?   ☐ Yes   ☐ No

Fire-safety education: ☐ In progress   ☐ Done   ☐ Not started   ☐ N/A

This session covered the following:

Covered	*Not covered*	
☐	☐	Began with joint meeting/check-in with child and caregiver
☐	☐	Reviewed previous home practice
☐	☐	Reviewed common antecedents to fire involvement
☐	☐	Got child's co-operation with caregiver monitoring of whereabouts
☐	☐	Developed skills with SNAP™: focus on thinking errors and thoughts that help
☐	☐	Ended with joint meeting with child and caregiver
☐	☐	Discussed home practice activities

Outcome of session:

☐ Next session scheduled for: _____

☐ Treatment terminated (client initiated)   ☐ Treatment terminated (clinician initiated)

Additional notes:

_____   _____

Signature/Credentials   Date

Choices and Consequences: Alternatives to Fire Involvement

Session at a glance

Background

While Session 3 focused on antecedents that may trigger (situations that may occur before) fire involvement, this session will focus on the role of consequences.

Like other behaviours, the child's fire involvement is responsive to the consequences that follow it. The consequences of fire involvement can include affective (emotional) arousal, excitement, feelings of relaxation, enjoyment of the characteristics of fire (colour, warmth, smell), positive peer regard, attention from caregivers, school suspension, loss of privileges, loss of property, and injury and legal charges, among other things. Some of these events (consequences) that follow fire involvement are positive and will increase the likelihood of future fire involvement, while other consequences are negative and will decrease the probability that the behaviour will occur again.

This session provides the child with the opportunity to explore any positive outcomes he or she has experienced as a result of involvement with fire and practise generating alternative ways of achieving these types of outcomes. Through additional practice with SNAP™, the child will continue to learn self-control and problem-solving skills. However, in this session, the child will focus on evaluating the likely consequences of choices and plans to further facilitate the use of fire-safe behaviours. The child should also leave Session 4 with a better understanding that his or her caregivers have a responsibility to respond to fire involvement in a way that decreases the likelihood of it occurring again.

The caregiver session will also focus on the consequences of fire involvement. Caregivers will explore common ineffective responses to their child's fire involvement, and will learn more about the characteristics of effective consequences and how to respond to future fire involvement.

By the end of the session, it is expected that the caregiver and child will agree upon a set of appropriate consequences for fire-related behaviours. This agreement will be formalized in a contract.

Goals

· Check in with the child and caregiver.

· Review the home practice activities with the child and caregiver.

· Identify the positive outcomes associated with fire involvement, and generate alternative ways to achieve similar outcomes.

· Discuss the caregiver's role in consequences.

· Use SNAP™ to evaluate choices and consequences.

· Wrap up and discuss the home practice activities with the child and caregiver.

If short of time

Your main goal is to continue the child's practice of SNAP™ skills, with an emphasis on the importance of thinking about likely consequences as a way of helping to make good decisions.

Materials needed

· blank white paper

· pencils

· coloured markers or pencil crayons

· stickers or other incentives

· Session 4 practice worksheets (p. 179)

· Session 4 progress note (p. 187)

Joint meeting with child and caregiver

Guidelines: 15 minutes

Clinician Note

The limits of confidentiality should be reviewed.

Check-in

⬛ **Have there been any further episodes of fire involvement since the last appointment?**

If no further fire involvement has been reported by the child or caregiver, assume the best and praise both participants for their efforts and good work.

If further fire involvement has occurred, model for the caregiver and child an appropriate response that includes recognizing the seriousness of this behaviour and the need for problem-solving to determine what went wrong as well as how to intervene further.

Ask the following question:

⬛ **Where is the family with regard to the Fire Services Education portion of TAPP-C?**

Review of home practice

Review the home practice from Session 3 with the child and caregiver. Ask the following questions:

⬛ **Did your family do the home check for ignition materials?**

⬛ **Did you (the caregiver) help the child practise SNAP™?**

⬛ **Did you (the caregiver) tell others who will be supervising the child about the child's fire involvement and about the fire-safety routines that will help?**

- **Did you work together to plan ahead regarding times the child would be without supervision?**

- **Did the family reward themselves for fire-safe behaviours?**

- **Did you use the *Safe Activities* worksheet (optional), p. 165, to make a list of activities that the child can do when unsupervised in the home or when in the community on his or her own?**

Was the family able to complete the home practice? If yes, praise their accomplishments and explore how they were able to get it done. If no, explore the obstacles, and encourage revisiting the assigned tasks. Use a collaborative problem-solving model when discussing how to accomplish the home practice tasks.

Child alone

Identify any positive outcomes associated with fire involvement, and generate alternative ways to achieve similar outcomes.

Guidelines: 10–15 minutes

Fire involvement serves a function for most children, whether it be a need for excitement, thrill-seeking, attention, revenge, taking the edge off of angry feelings, or reducing anxiety, to name just a few.

The more the child continues to experience positive consequences from his or her fire involvement, the greater the possibility that the fire-related behaviour will continue.

The aim of the following exercise is to identify any positive outcomes of fire involvement, and to target alternative and safer strategies that will fulfil the same or similar functions for the child.

For children that are having difficulty with this task, it may be helpful for the clinician to review concrete examples of the child's recent fire-related incidents in order to highlight any positive outcomes the fire involvement may have brought the child.

The clinician may want to say something like: "We have already discussed the dangers and other negative consequences associated with fire involvement. Now let's talk about some reasons why children may like fire."

Use the following questions to begin a discussion with the child. Complete Part 1 of the Positive Outcomes of Fire Involvement *worksheet.*

- **What are some things that make matches, lighters or fire-play attractive to children?**

- **What kinds of things happen that make them want to try it again?**

- **Is there something that happens to you that makes you want to try it again?**

Use the following questions to engage the child as a collaborator by helping him or her think of alternative activities or behaviours that could serve the same function(s) or bring the same positive outcomes as the fire involvement. Let the child know that his or her caregiver will also be responsible for brainstorming ideas to share during the joint wrap-up at the end of the session. Complete Part 2 of the Positive Outcomes of Fire Involvement *worksheet.*

- **What other safe ways could children and teens achieve similar outcomes?**

- **Is there something your caregiver could do to help you use these other behaviours instead of the fire involvement?**

- **Is there something you have done in the past as an alternative to fire involvement?**

- **What's the hardest thing about doing something differently? The easiest?**

Discuss the caregiver's role concerning consequences.

Guidelines: 10–15 minutes

In Session 4, the caregiver will be learning how to identify ineffective caregiver consequences or responses to the child's fire involvement, as well as building skills to select appropriate consequences. By developing a proactive plan with the clinician, the caregiver will be reducing the likelihood that she or he will under- or overreact to a fire-related incident.

The goal of the proactive plan is to increase the likelihood that the caregiver's consequence is consistent, predictable and meaningful.

Use the following questions to begin a discussion with the child about the caregiver's role with regard to consequences. Through discussion, highlight the connection between effective consequences and stopping the fire involvement. Help to prepare the child for a subsequent discussion about consequences with the caregiver during the joint meeting. Inform the child that the caregiver will come to the joint meeting to share the plan, and that the child's input will be requested.

- **Why is it important for a caregiver to provide consequences to a child who has been involved with fire?**

- **What is likely to happen if the child does not receive a meaningful consequence?**

- **What kinds of consequences might help a child stop the fire involvement?**

- **What kinds of things can a caregiver do when a child breaks an important rule?**

- **What kinds of consequences seemed to work for you (the child) in the past?**

- **What kinds of consequences did not work for you (the child) in the past? Why not? (e.g., Did the caregiver follow through? Was the consequence meaningful?)**

Use SNAP™ to identify choices and consequences.

Guidelines: 30–40 minutes

This section focuses on helping the child to use SNAP™ to think more deliberately and proactively about the consequences of his or her choices or plans.

The child will get additional practice using SNAP™ to stop him- or herself from touching an ignition source and for planning other things to do instead. The emphasis in this session, however, will be on evaluating the likely consequences of choices as a way of helping to make good decisions.

Using the *Choices/Consequences* worksheet, have the child generate a list of action choices when faced with finding a lighter on the ground outside his or her home. Encourage the child to brainstorm as many possible choices as he or she can (including choices that will result in negative consequences; for example, picking up the lighter to play with it).

Next, assist the child in generating the likely consequences for each choice. For older children, the clinician can facilitate a discussion around short- and long-term consequences. For example, the clinician can help the child reflect on the short- (e.g., suspension from school) and long-term (e.g., the effect of suspensions on the school record, learning, achievement and post high school) consequences of fire involvement at school.

As in earlier sessions, the clinician may first model the SNAP™ skills through role-play and video, and then assist the child in enacting the skills during a role-play. Based on what you know about the child (antecedents to and patterns of fire involvement), help the child set up a *relevant* hypothetical vignette to have him or her practise the new skills in the session, focusing more specifically on the PLAN: choices and consequences.

> *The clinician can role-play the following scenario and use the questions that follow to guide the child's thinking and problem-solving.*

Scenario

"Well, I'm sitting here in my room. I've already tried to keep myself busy. I've listened to the radio (played with toys, etc.) and now I'm bored. Maybe it would be fun to sneak my mom's lighter from her purse and play with it."

- **What is the problem facing the child?**
- **What kinds of thoughts are going through his or her head?**
- **How does the child feel?**
- **What is the first thing the child needs to do? (Use SNAP™.)**
- **How can the child STOP him- or herself from going to find the lighter?**
- **What kinds of thoughts might help?**

Demonstrate SNAP™.

The clinician SNAPS her fingers, and counts to 10 (or whatever has worked for the child in the past).

> *Aloud, the clinician generates a number of choices for behaviours that he or she can do instead of going to find the lighter.*

Scenario

"Well, I could actually try to sneak the lighter. I could go and let my mom know that I am bored. I could go bother my brother. Or I could go downstairs and ask my mom if I can go to my friend's house."

At this point, the clinician can "freeze" the role-play, and have the child assist her in stating the likely consequences associated with each choice (either by taking turns or having the child instruct the clinician as to the appropriate consequences). Once the child has helped the clinician review the choices and consequences, the clinician can carry on the role-play and make an informed choice, based on the likely consequences.

The child can also assist in evaluating the problem-solving process and the chosen course of action.

Help the child to select another scenario (possibly one the child has had difficulty with) and incorporate it into a role-play, focusing on choices and consequences. The clinician may wish to complete the *SNAP™ In-Session Practice* worksheet with the child.

Remind the child that he or she will be asked to teach the caregiver about SNAP™, and practise the SNAP™ skills at home or in the community before the next session (i.e., when a problem or potential problem arises, use SNAP™ to generate choices and select one of the safe alternatives).

The following are a few ideas for variations on in-session practice.

The child and clinician can continue to act out relevant scenarios. Both participants have the option of "freezing" the role-play to make suggestions.

Once a role-play has been completed, the two participants may reverse roles to facilitate perspective-taking skills.

Videotape the child attempting a role-play. Review the tape and have the child evaluate it. After self-evaluation and feedback from the clinician, the child may redo the scenario using a revised strategy, a new coping skill, or an added choice.

Wrap-up and joint meeting with child and caregiver

Guidelines: 15 minutes

Have the child and caregiver share their ideas about the functions or positive things the fire involvement may be bringing the child, and their ideas about alternative and safer ways of achieving those outcomes. Are there any additional things either the caregiver or the child could do to help achieve these outcomes in more appropriate ways?

Ask the caregiver to explain to the child the way that he or she will be dealing with any future fire involvement. Have the caregiver go through the steps she or he will use. Solicit the child's views about the suggested consequences. Does the child have any suggestions regarding consequences that would work for him or her?

Have the child demonstrate the use of SNAP™, and ask him or her to think out loud about the likely consequences of his or her choice of different plans or behaviours (e.g., looking for a lighter versus doing something else). The child can also inform the caregiver about an alternative strategy that will be attempted before the next session.

Finish the session by drafting a contract stating that the child has agreed that he or she will no longer play with fire and the agreed on caregiver response and consequence for any further fire involvement. Have the caregiver and child sign it and the clinician witness it.

Discuss home practice.

The following are the suggested home practice activities to be completed before the next session:

1. The caregiver should post the contract in an obvious place in the home, such as on the door of the fridge.

2. The caregiver and the child should check the home for ignition materials and update the previously completed *Home Fire-Safety Search* worksheet, p. 22.

3. The caregiver should help the child practise SNAP™ on two occasions: one on paper (see the *SNAP™ Tracking Sheets)* and one through a role-play focusing on identifying choices and consequences. (The caregiver and child can also discuss how SNAP™ can be used for any situations that have occurred or will likely occur before the next session). The caregiver should sign off on this home practice activity.

4. Once a day until the next session, the caregiver should sit with the child and plan for times that day or the following day that the child will be out of caregiver's view or unsupervised. Together they should complete the *Times without Supervision* worksheet.

5. The caregiver should reward the child for fire-safe behaviours.

6. The caregiver should help the child complete the *Home Practice Checklist*, p. 186, by checking off the tasks the child has completed.

Choices and Consequences:
Alternatives to Fire Involvement

Date: _____

Positive Outcomes of Fire Involvement

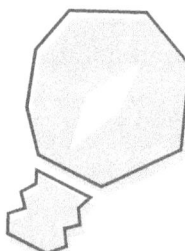

Part 1

What are some of the positive outcomes of fire involvement that you have experienced (or that you can imagine)?

1._____

2._____

3._____

4._____

5._____

Part 2

What are some alternative activities that could achieve similar positive outcomes?

1._____

2._____

3._____

4._____

5._____

Choices/Consequences

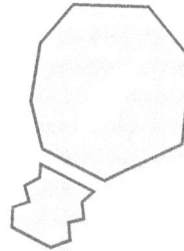

When you find a lighter on the ground outside of your home, what are your *action choices?*

What are the likely consequences *for each of your choices?*

1._____

2._____

3._____

4._____

1._____

2._____

3._____

4._____

SNAP™ In-Session Practice

Date: _____

Scenario:

_____

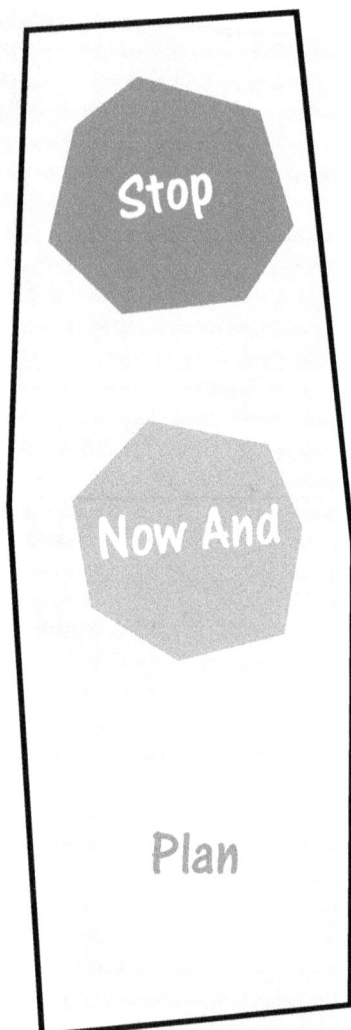

1. Ways I can stop myself (fill out the wheel of self-control)

_____

_____

_____

2. Thoughts that will help

_____

_____

_____

3. Things I can do instead (fill out the wheel of plans)

_____

_____

_____

SNAP™ Tracking Sheet

Name: _____ Date: _____

What time of day was it? ☐ Morning ☐ Afternoon ☐ Evening ☐ Nighttime

Where was I? ☐ Home ☐ School ☐ Community

Who was I with? ☐ Alone ☐ Friends ☐ Brother/Sister ☐ Caregiver

What happened? _____

How was I feeling? _____

What was I thinking? _____

Ways I stopped myself...

1 _____ 2 _____ 3 _____

Thoughts that helped...

1 _____ 2 _____ 3 _____

My plan was...

1 _____ 2 _____ 3 _____

How did I do?

I made my problem...   ☐ Smaller   ☐ Same   ☐ Bigger

My caregiver's signature: _____

SNAP™ Tracking Sheet

Name: _____ Date: _____

What time of day was it? ☐ Morning ☐ Afternoon ☐ Evening ☐ Nighttime

Where was I? ☐ Home ☐ School ☐ Community

Who was I with? ☐ Alone ☐ Friends ☐ Brother/Sister ☐ Caregiver

What happened? _____

How was I feeling? _____

What was I thinking? _____

Ways I stopped myself...

1 _____ 2 _____ 3 _____

Thoughts that helped...

1 _____ 2 _____ 3 _____

My plan was...

1 _____ 2 _____ 3 _____

How did I do?

I made my problem... ☐ Smaller ☐ Same ☐ Bigger

My caregiver's signature: _____

Times
without
Supervision

Answer the questions to help plan for times the child will be without supervision:

When will the child be
without supervision? _____

Where will
the child be? _____

What will the
child be doing? _____

Who will be
with the child? _____

Is access to ignition
materials a concern? _____

Check in time: When
should I check in with my child? _____

Things the caregiver can do
to keep the child safe: _____

Things the child can do that
would help keep him- or herself safe: _____

Home Practice Checklist

1. Help your caregiver post the Home Fire-Safety Search worksheet and the contract.

   Check and date completed: _____

2. Help your caregiver check before the next session that matches and lighters are being kept as planned (twice).

   Check and date completed: _____   Check and date completed: _____

3. Practise SNAP™ (twice).

   Check and date completed: _____   Check and date completed: _____

4. Plan for times without supervision.

   Check and date completed: _____   Check and date completed: _____

   Check and date completed: _____   Check and date completed: _____

   Check and date completed: _____   Check and date completed: _____

   Check and date completed: _____   Check and date completed: _____

5. Were you rewarded for your fire-safety efforts?

   Check and date completed: _____

Choices and Consequences:
Alternatives to Fire Involvement

Name: _____ File no.: _____ Session date: _____

Action plan:

☐ Client cancelled (specify action plan)   _____

☐ No show (specify action plan)   _____

☐ Clinician cancelled (specify action plan)   _____

☐ Attended Session 4 of the TAPP-C program

Fire involvement since last session?   ☐ Yes   ☐ No

Fire-safety education: ☐ In progress   ☐ Done   ☐ Not started   ☐ N/A

This session covered the following:

Covered   *Not covered*

☐	☐	Began with joint meeting/check-in with child and caregiver
☐	☐	Reviewed previous home practice
☐	☐	Identified the positive outcomes associated with fire involvement and generated alternative ways to achieve similar outcomes
☐	☐	Discussed the caregiver's role in providing consequences
☐	☐	Used SNAP™ to evaluate choices and consequences
☐	☐	Ended with joint meeting with child and caregiver
☐	☐	Discussed home practice activities

Additional notes:

_____   _____
Signature/Credentials   Date

Session 5

Child

Termination: Reviewing Fire-Safe Behaviours and Recognizing the Child's Accomplishments

Session at a glance

Background

The final session provides an opportunity to review the issues covered and progress made in the previous sessions, and to develop a relapse prevention plan should fire involvements re-occur. It also provides an opportunity to

· discuss the termination of the TAPP-C intervention

· formally recognize the completion of the TAPP-C program

· discuss any further interventions that are recommended for the child and/or family.

Goals

· Check in.

· Review home practice activities with the child and caregiver.

· Discuss termination issues.

· Review progress made.

· Develop a relapse prevention plan.

· Meet with the child and caregiver to review main points of the treatment intervention, as well as to highlight and address any further intervention needed.

· Recognize the completion of the TAPP-C program.

If short for time

Your main goals are to discuss termination issues, to review the proactive plans to prevent future fire involvement, and to facilitate any referrals for ongoing or supplemental intervention.

Materials needed

- · blank white paper
- · pencils
- · stickers or other incentives
- · Certificate of Completion (p. 199)
- · video camera (optional), blank video tape, VCR and monitor or audiotape recorder[4]
- · Session 5 progress note (p. 201)
- · reward (if applicable)
- · consent forms to contact other agencies, if necessary

Joint meeting with child and caregiver

Guidelines: 15 minutes

Clinician Note

The limits of confidentiality should be reviewed.

Check-in

Have there been any further episodes of fire involvement since the last appointment?

If no further fire involvement has been reported by the child or caregiver, assume the best and praise both participants for their efforts and good work.

If further fire involvement has occurred, model for the child and caregiver an appropriate response that includes recognizing the seriousness of this behaviour and the need for problem-solving to determine what went wrong, as well as how to intervene further.

---

[4] It will be useful to have some type of equipment to record the child's final exercise.

Ask the following question:

- **Where is your family with regard to the Fire Services Education portion of TAPP-C?**

Review of home practice

Review the home practice activity from the previous session. Be sure to use praise liberally for effort, rather than for success.

If problems arose, work with the child to amend the home practice activity so as to maximize the child's chances for success.

Keep in mind that it is optimal to add intervention sessions until the child has had an opportunity to experience at least partial success in each of the home practice activities.

Ask the following questions:

- **Did the family post the contract?**
- **Did the family search/monitor the home for ignition materials?**
- **Is the family keeping ignition materials in the agreed upon ways?**
- **Did the caregiver help the child practise SNAP™?**
- **Did the family plan for times without supervision?**
- **Did the family reward themselves for using the fire-safety behaviours?**

Child alone

Discuss termination issues.

Guidelines: 10 minutes

For most children, this will be the last face-to-face intervention session. However, some children and adolescents may require further weekly sessions or periodic booster sessions in order to continue skill development and practice.

If this is the final session, ask the child how she or he is feeling about finishing up. Modify the discussion depending on how the child is thinking and feeling about termination (e.g., some children may feel sad, while others will be more than happy to conclude their sessions).

Regardless of the child's reaction to the final session, the clinician should continue to communicate warmth and acceptance, to show recognition for the child's efforts, and to reinforce any positive changes that have taken place. For example, let the child know that you enjoyed working with him or her.

Communicate your own feelings about the final session; for example, that you are sad to see the sessions end, but that you are happy that the child has learned some new skills.

Be specific with your praise regarding the child's progress to date, highlighting occasions when the child exhibited notable effort or mastered specific fire-safe behaviours or strategies.

Answer any questions or concerns that the child may have with regard to termination.

While discussing termination issues, be sure to tell the child to expect a one-month follow-up phone call and let him or her know about any future fire-specific intervention plans. Let the child know that, although this is the last face-to-face meeting, you will be thinking about him or her. Explain that phone contact is a good way for you to monitor his or her progress, and to work together regarding any further problem-solving if necessary.

Also, inform the child that you will give your office phone number to the child's caregiver, so that either one can reach you with any questions or concerns about fire involvement that may arise in the future.

Review progress

Guidelines: 20 minutes

Briefly review with the child his or her general progress over the course of the intervention. For example, ask the child's ideas, thoughts and feelings on the following topics. (Refer to practice worksheets completed throughout the intervention.)

Main lessons of TAPP-C

· the perceived strengths and/or areas in need of improvement

· the strategies that seemed to work best for the child

· the situations in the future where the child may likely have to use his or her new skills and

· any obstacles to using new fire-safe behaviours and coping skills

Once the clinician has gained an understanding of the child's perceptions, this can easily lead into a follow-up discussion around these topics. For example, does the clinician have similar thoughts and/or ideas around these issues? Are there any areas in which the clinician's thoughts or ideas differ? Does the clinician have anything to add with regard to strengths, coping strategies, situational factors or obstacles?

Make a plan to deal with high-risk situations and firesetting urges that may arise in the future.

Guidelines: 30 minutes

At this stage of the intervention, the child should be able to identify the likely antecedents to his or her fire involvement (including internal and external factors). As well, the child will have learned and practised a variety of fire-safe behaviours and skills devised to manage risks for further fire involvement.

The clinician will need to use this information to help the child articulate a plan to manage risk for further fire involvement. Because the content of this plan will vary depending on the presenting issues of each child, future planning with the child will probably take some combination of clinical judgment and creativity in order to develop a plan that works best for the child and the caregiver.

While developing this plan with the child, keep in mind that the overriding goal is to maximize the generalizability and maintenance of any positive changes that may have resulted from participation in the treatment component of TAPP-C (i.e., the treatment effects).

Empirical work on juvenile firesetters indicates that recidivism is quite common. Therefore, in developing a relapse prevention plan with the child, you will want to normalize any future difficulties that the child may have in terms of applying fire-safe behaviours and skills in real-life situations. For example, the clinician might explain that the child cannot expect the urges and precipitants for fire involvement to "go away overnight." Instead, communicate that it is a matter of managing these urges and situations with the skills that the child has learned from TAPP-C.

Let the child know that, although it may seem tough now, these skills will probably come more easily over time with lots of practice.

Remind the child that someone has been working with the caregiver so that he or she can assist the child with these skills (i.e., the child is not alone in this process). The important message that the child should take home is that these TAPP-C skills take time to perfect, as well as a great deal of practice and support from others.

The following are some questions that the clinician might consider asking the child in her discussion around future planning:

- **In your opinion, how likely is it that you'll become involved with fire (e.g., play with matches or lighters or start a fire) in the future?**

- **What would be your first sign that you may be heading for trouble?**

- **Who are you likely to be with when you become involved with fire?**

- **Where are you likely to be when you become involved with fire?**

- **At what time of day are you more likely to become involved with fire?**

- **What thoughts are you likely to have prior to becoming involved with fire?**

- **What feelings are you likely to have prior to becoming involved with fire?**

- **What are your options once you realize that you have the urge to become involved with fire?**

- **What skills can you use to *stop* yourself from becoming involved with fire?**

- **With whom can you talk if you get the urge?**

- **How can your caregiver help you?**

- **Who else can help you?**

- **What would you need from them?**

- **What is your responsibility and theirs?**

- **If you were to become involved with fire in the future, what type of consequences would you expect from your caregiver?**

The following are a couple of ideas for exercises to help the child solidify his or her commitment to using fire-safe behaviours:

· Film the child acting out a commercial about the TAPP-C program, with the goal of helping other children avoid fire involvement. Have the child talk about the interventions he or she found most helpful or have the child demonstrate using SNAP™ in realistic fire-related scenarios that may arise.

· Help the child create a song, poem, story or picture that highlights the interventions that the child found most helpful. Tape-record the song, poem or story, if possible.

Wrap-up and joint meeting with child and caregiver
Guidelines: 15 minutes

Assist the child and caregiver in reviewing their relapse plans with each other. Ensure that the roles and responsibilities of both child and caregiver are clear, and that the caregiver will be able to provide adequate assistance and support for the child's ongoing efforts.

Discuss possible recommendations for future interventions or referrals to other programs or services, as needed.

Help the child share the commercial, song, poem, story or picture that he or she created.

Discuss the child's accomplishments and the caregiver's accomplishments.

To recognize the child's accomplishments, present the child with the reward that he or she has earned. The reward may be a certificate or a standard item or gift that the clinician uses with all clients, or it may be a reward specifically tailored to that child. For instance, the reward may be something tangible or intangible that has been decided on in advance in consultation with the caregiver.

Present the family with a *Certificate of Completion.*

Clinician Note

Regardless of the length and manner of celebration, be sure to thank the caregiver for his or her help and support and to communicate to the child how pleased you are with his or her efforts and accomplishments.

Termination:
Reviewing Fire-Safe Behaviours and Recognizing the Child's Accomplishments

Date: _____

Certificate of Completion

For hard work and effort at becoming fire-safe

Names of participants:

_____

_____

Date: _____

Program representative signature:

_____

TAPP-C
Progress Note

Child

Termination:
Reviewing Fire-Safe Behaviours and
Recognizing the Child's Accomplishments

Name: _____   File no.: _____   Session date: _____

Action plan:

☐ Client cancelled (specify action plan)   _____

☐ No show (specify action plan)   _____

☐ Clinician cancelled (specify action plan)   _____

☐ Attended Session 5 of the TAPP-C program

Fire involvement since last session?   ☐ Yes   ☐ No

Fire-safety education: ☐ In progress   ☐ Done   ☐ Not started   ☐ N/A

This session covered the following:

Covered   *Not covered*

☐   ☐   Began with joint meeting/check-in with child and caregiver

☐   ☐   Reviewed previous home practice

☐   ☐   Discussed termination issues

☐   ☐   Reviewed progress over course of intervention

☐   ☐   Planned for management of future risks

☐   ☐   Ended with joint meeting with child and caregiver

☐   ☐   Presented Certificate or reward

Additional notes:

_____   _____
Signature/Credentials   Date

Part 4

TAPP-C

The reluctant or resistant caregiver

Considerations

As a clinician, you will invariably encounter caregivers who indicate either an inability or reluctance to follow through with intervention suggestions, such as home searches for fire materials, restricting access to ignition sources, and/or increasing the supervision of the child. In these instances, it is important to explore with the caregiver the reasons for the apprehension or reluctance to complete the assigned tasks or intervention recommendations.

For instance, if a caregiver's reluctance to comply with treatment recommendations is a motivation issue, find ways to engage the caregiver in the treatment, and help him or her to understand the importance of fire safety.

Likewise, some caregivers may not feel a specific intervention is necessary in their home or for their child. Discussing this openly with the caregiver may help clarify any (mis)conceptions they have about fire-related behaviour.

Others may feel unable to succeed with an intervention, expecting that their child will not comply or that they do not have the resources to meet certain treatment requests.

Another common complaint that caregivers voice is the lack of time or energy to complete certain interventions.

The parents of children who engage in firesetting often have limited resources to cope with the demands of their daily life, and feel overwhelmed. To ask them to perform further household and parenting tasks (like searching the home for fire materials and increasing the supervision of their child) can often strain an already weary parent. Part of the clinician's job is to access the caregiver's internal resources and build in more external resources so that they can follow through on necessary interventions. Asking the caregiver who else in his or her life may be able to help institute various recommendations is often a beginning to making a fire-safety treatment plan with a caregiver.

Intervention modifications

For instance, supervision is often an issue for working parents in the late afternoon, after their child returns home from school but before the parent gets home from work. The clinician could use a problem-solving approach with the caregiver to brainstorm a number of supervision possibilities for the child during the late afternoon. Drawing on extended family members, family friends and neighbours, or taking advantage of after-school groups or structured activities are often viable supervision alternatives when caregivers are unavailable.

Another practical suggestion for supervising children is to establish a "safe" area in the home in which the child can play, and not be directly supervised by an adult. It is imperative that the "safe" area be void of any fire materials, as well as other potential safety hazards, so that the caregiver can take care of other demands or duties in the home while the child is allowed to play safely.

The clinician will need to work collaboratively with the caregiver to understand the nature of the resistance or reluctance, break down the problem or obstacle into manageable pieces, and use a problem-solving approach to develop strategies to implement needed intervention.

In addition to the direct benefits of the fire-safety interventions themselves, following through on such interventions sends an important message to the child or teenager that fire safety is important in the family's home. It also allows the caregiver to model fire-safe behaviour.

In an effort to prevent obstacles from interfering with a caregiver's (or child's) participation in the program, and to increase the family's chances of success, it is helpful to continuously ask for client input, especially regarding the likelihood of their being able to implement the suggested interventions. Treatment recommendations can then be adapted accordingly.

Religious, spiritual and cultural fire-related practices

Considerations

Many families may engage in fire-related activities associated with their religious, spiritual and/or cultural beliefs and practices. These activities may include burning candles, sweetgrass, incense or other materials on a regular basis and/or for long periods of time.

These activities increase a child's risk for fire involvement because they require the availability of ignition sources, and the burning materials themselves may be used as ignition sources.

Moreover, families may not immediately view these activities as potentially risky, since they may have engaged in them for many years and/or many times without any difficulty. Caregivers may also mistakenly assume that children would never misuse something of great value or sacredness.

Fire is dangerous regardless of the meaning assigned to it and must be handled safely.

Intervention modifications

Religious, spiritual and/or cultural fire-related practices are important to consider in the intervention process. These practices should be viewed as positive uses of fire.

These activities provide opportunities for caregivers to model appropriate fire-related behaviours, particularly fire-safe behaviours. Caregivers can use these practices as opportunities to articulate the fire-safety measures they are taking, thereby modelling fire-safe attitudes and behaviour. As well, if the practices have positive fire-related teachings associated with them, these may be shared with children, if appropriate.

Caregivers should be encouraged to find out how to practise their activity in the safest way possible; for example, candles that will be burning for a long period of time need to be in sturdy, non-flammable candle holders in safe, stable locations.

They may benefit from consulting with their local fire service professional about safe ways to conduct these fire-related activities.

Since access to fire materials is not likely to be completely eliminated in situations where fire is being used as part of religious, spiritual and/or cultural practices, supervision of the child becomes especially important.

Children should never be left unsupervised in the presence of burning materials. Children should, however, be encouraged to participate in religious and/or cultural fire-related practices with appropriate fire-safety measures and adult supervision in place.

Rural and remote communities

Considerations

In rural and remote communities, children may be more exposed to fire-related activities, such as burning garbage, fire pits and wood stoves for household heating.

Children may also be more likely to have greater access to fire, fire-related materials and accelerants. Indeed, they may be expected to routinely use fire or fire-related materials as part of household responsibilities, and/or they may be taught to carry matches or lighters for safety or survival.

Caregivers and other community members may perceive the notion of attempting to limit access to fire materials as unrealistic and even impossible because of extensive reliance on such materials in daily life and their ready availability throughout the community.

Intervention modifications

Restricting access is still a fundamental component of any intervention to reduce fire involvement by children and teens.

Special attention should be paid to working collaboratively with parents in order to determine an access restriction plan that is *workable* for the family. If it is unlikely that the child's access to fire materials can be restricted, especially in the community, then it may be necessary to work with the family to ensure high levels of supervision.

It may also be especially important to involve other adults from the community with whom the family is connected in order to develop an effective plan. Moreover, some education may need to take place at the community level to address community attitudes toward restricting access to fire materials.

While it is essential to emphasize restricting access in the short term, it is also important to plan how to gradually reintroduce fire-related responsibilities as soon as is appropriate. Reintroduction should be done in a planned, supervised manner.

The clinician should become familiar with resources available in the family's community, if necessary.

Group homes and residential facilities

Considerations

Group homes and residential treatment facilities present both special advantages and special challenges for managing children and youth who have been involved with fire. Many facilities have the capacity to provide high levels of supervision and control over materials in a child or youth's living environment. In addition, they may provide children and youth with planned, positive fire-related activities. Lastly, they offer opportunities to integrate modifying fire-related behaviour into already existing behaviour-modification plans.

As children with severe difficulties are more likely to have been involved in fire-related behaviours, it is quite likely that there will be more than one

firesetter in a particular facility at a given time. These youth may work together to circumvent measures put in place to reduce fire involvement and may exacerbate each other's conditions. They may continue to perpetuate anti-social fire related beliefs and attitudes and work together to disrupt efforts to emphasize fire-safe beliefs, attitudes and behaviours.

In addition to these difficulties, these facilities are sometimes staffed by young, relatively inexperienced people who may have very little clinical training. Some of the staff may themselves have inappropriate beliefs and attitudes about fire safety and fire-related behaviours. For example, in one situation that came to clinical attention, a group home staff member showed a youth how to explode aerosol cans in a campfire. Other examples include group home staff failing to take fire drills seriously, smoking with residents, showing residents lighter tricks and/or leaving fire materials accessible.

Intervention modifications

All of the interventions designed to be used in family homes should also occur in group home and residential facilities. If a child is having weekend visits at the family home, or the intention is to have the child eventually return to the family home, the interventions should also be used in the family home.

Fire-safety routines will benefit all children in a facility, not just the children involved with fire.

Group home staff should receive training on the importance and implementation of fire-safety procedures. Fire-safety procedures need to be followed routinely and reviewed with each new resident and staff person as soon as they move into the facility, not just in response to the admission of a juvenile firesetter.

In the group home, fire materials should be locked at all times, except when they are being used by staff or residents under direct staff supervision. This includes cigarettes, as lit cigarettes can be used to ignite other materials.

The group home should have a smoking policy for staff and residents, and all staff should receive training in implementing the smoking policy. Cigarette lighters should be removed from group home vehicles used by residents.

All resident responsibilities and chores should also be examined to ensure that residents are not intentionally or unintentionally given access to fire-starting materials, such as gasoline for the lawnmower or flammable cleaning products.

Fire-safe behaviour, such as checking to ensure the escape plan is posted and practised, that the smoke alarms are working, and that exits are clear, should be integrated into existing chore routines and rewarded with praise and other appropriate reinforcers.

Fire-dangerous behaviour, including possessing fire materials and/or providing fire materials to others should be integrated into existing behaviour-management plans and responded to with appropriate consequences.

Children and youth with histories of fire involvement should not have unsupervised access to each other.

Comorbid conditions

Considerations

Fire involvement typically occurs in the context of other psychopathology or difficulties. Accordingly, it is essential that children and youth involved with fire receive a comprehensive assessment not only of their fire involvement, but also of their general mental health needs.

In the context of disruptive or anti-social behavioural difficulties, fire involvement may be just one example of many difficult behaviours that the child is exhibiting.

Often, fire involvement occurs in the context of difficulties with impulsivity. In rarer circumstances, fire involvement may be part of a mood

and/or thought disorder. Sometimes fire may be used as a self-harming technique. At other times, fire involvement may occur in the context of pervasive developmental disorders or limited intellectual functioning. A child or youth may also develop symptoms of post-traumatic stress following a particularly serious fire episode.

Intervention modifications

Despite the presence of other difficulties or conditions, restricting access to fire materials and improving supervision and monitoring of the child are still key to eliminating fire involvement in the short term. This ensures the safety of the child, allowing caregivers and others to focus on the child's other mental health needs. Appropriate treatment for other difficulties should reduce the likelihood of further fire involvement. Appropriate referrals for additional treatment should be facilitated, as appropriate.

In situations where a child's fire involvement has resulted in significant trauma to the child, it may be necessary to reduce, delay or eliminate some of the child treatment components. It is important, however, that the caregiver treatment component proceed.

Preschoolers

Considerations

Preschoolers are more likely to be injured or killed by fire than older children, adolescents and adults.

They are at increased risk because of their poor understanding of the consequences of fire, limited ability to escape from fire, smaller body size and more sensitive skin.

They may play with matches or fire in enclosed spaces, such as under a bed, behind a sofa or in a closet where fires are more likely to start and more likely to spread quickly and where escape is less likely.

In addition, caregivers may underestimate their preschoolers' capacity for seeking out and using fire-related materials, because they are perceived as too young to engage in these behaviours. Thus, it is important to view fire involvement by preschoolers as an especially high-risk and concerning behaviour in need of immediate attention.

Intervention modifications

Increased emphasis on parental interventions

Caregivers need to be made aware of the heightened risk for injury faced by their young children, and the need for them to take immediate and comprehensive action. Caregivers of preschoolers may need to be reminded that it is not developmentally appropriate to expect a preschooler to not touch fire materials that are available in the environment. Instead, it is absolutely essential that caregivers take responsibility for eliminating their children's access to fire materials.

Because preschoolers are not usually in the community unsupervised, their access to fire materials is often limited to residential settings. Successful implementation of access restriction strategies in these settings can be very effective at eliminating fire involvement.

Since preschoolers may engage in fire involvement in enclosed spaces, it may be necessary to suggest unconventional interventions, such as removal of the closet door, removal of the contents of a closet, installation of a smoke alarm in the closet (or other enclosed locations of fire involvement) or putting a lock on the door to the furnace room or basement.

Cooking fires started by unsupervised preschoolers can be a red flag for inadequate, perhaps neglectful supervision by a caregiver. In such situations, the clinician should investigate other unsafe and dangerous behaviours secondary to inadequate caregiver supervision. Associated unsafe behaviours might include wandering, dangerous climbing, ingestion of chemicals or medication, poisonings and playing with unsafe implements such as knives. Involving child welfare authorities is often warranted in such cases.

Preschoolers' limited understanding of fire, as well as their physical and mobility needs, require special attention to home fire escape planning. Caregivers should take responsibility for developing an appropriate escape plan to ensure their preschoolers' exit from a house fire. Fire service professionals can assist with this escape plan.

Increased need to ensure that parents follow through with intervention

Since preschoolers are at high risk for serious injury and/or death due to fire involvement, it is important from a child welfare perspective that caregivers participate in interventions to eliminate this behaviour.

It may be necessary to involve child protection authorities if caregivers are unwilling or unable to follow through with interventions to eliminate their child's fire involvement.

Simplification or elimination of child intervention

Depending on the developmental level of the child, it may be necessary to greatly simplify and/or eliminate the child intervention. For example, it is likely not appropriate to attempt the child treatment component with a three-year-old. Again, this increases the importance of comprehensive work with caregivers.

Adolescents

While we have indicated that this manual is perhaps better suited for use with school-aged children, our experience over the years has shown that the intervention methods outlined are also useful and quite successful for adolescents as well. However, several considerations need to be made when working with adolescents.

Considerations

Clinical issues that distinguish adolescents from children often include adolescents' greater resistance to intervention, their level of maturity and need for independence, less stringent supervision, greater access to fire materials outside of the home, peer influences and peer pressure, and opportunity to smoke and subsequent need to carry matches and lighters.

Furthermore, it is important to note that many adolescents with histories of fire involvement also exhibit other antisocial behaviours and have had some contact with the legal system.

Intervention modifications

In contrast to younger children, adolescents seem initially to be more resistant to intervention. However, ensuring the following general steps are taken often helps to reduce the adolescent's reluctance to participate in the program and motivates them to alter their fire-related behaviour:

1. Make sure that they understand that the interventions are not punishments and can actually help keep them out of trouble in the future.

2. Identify individual motivators to eliminate fire involvement.

3. Ensure that specific intervention strategies and case examples are relevant to them.

4. Establish a collaborative relationship with them, encouraging their input and direction regarding the course of treatment.

Given that adolescents are typically granted more freedom, supervised less often, and have greater access to fire materials than children, it is particularly important to have the adolescents motivated to change their fire-related behaviour.

Engaging the adolescent in treatment may present some challenges. While getting acquainted with the youth during the initial portions of the program, the clinician should attempt to identify key motivators for their adolescent client. For instance, many teenagers are tired of getting into trouble for their behaviour, and wish to avoid

(further) contact with the law. Others are motivated to keep themselves or family members safe. The first, and often the most difficult, step in working with adolescents involved with fire is to help them understand that altering their fire-related behaviour may help them achieve certain goals (such as staying out of trouble).

The clinician will want to adapt the SNAP™ program for use with older and more mature individuals. For instance, a greater focus on problem-solving strategies may be more applicable to adolescents. Hypothetical vignettes presented to adolescents to practise problem-solving skills during sessions should be relevant to the individual adolescent and his or her life experiences.

Scenarios may include situations involving peers and the social pressure to participate in fire involvement within a group, how to handle the wider access to fire materials outside of the home (e.g., in stores), and issues inherent to smoking cigarettes (e.g., asking for someone to light their cigarette or to borrow a lighter rather than carry one).

It is important to encourage adolescents' input on intervention suggestions throughout treatment, and to work collaboratively with them. For instance, if an adolescent indicates that a specific intervention is not realistic, or he or she disagrees with a recommendation, it is imperative to explore this with him or her.

A common complaint from adolescents who smoke is the recommendation that they refrain from carrying matches or lighters to light their cigarettes. They often report this is an excessive and unnecessary limitation. A strategy that has met with some success is to have the adolescents see how this restriction could actually work for them. For instance, many of these youth report being frustrated in the past for being blamed for offences they did not commit. They also recognize that they are likely to become a suspect for any future fire-related offence given their fire history. Inform them that if they never carry matches or lighters (and refrain from other fire involvement), they are less likely to be blamed for future fire-related transgressions in their neighbourhood.

Ultimately, you as the clinician may feel strongly about a particular recommendation to which the adolescent remains opposed, but it is important that the adolescent has a voice in his or her treatment and feels listened to and respected.

It is often appropriate to allow older youth some involvement with sanctioned fire-related practices. Clinical judgment will determine the extent of supervision needed for such fire contact. Some common examples are adolescents helping to safely start a campfire with caregiver supervision, or cooking using a stove or barbecue. Such appropriate fire-related activities should be planned and agreed upon by the caregiver.

For families with an adolescent involved with fire, working directly with the youth is vital for behavioural change. However, it remains important to also involve the youth's caregiver in treatment. Although some caregivers report having little control over their teen's behaviour and access to fire materials outside of the home, they can still convey the message that fire involvement is a serious matter, and that fire safety is an important family goal.

Furthermore, when working with caregivers who indicate being unable to supervise their teenager because he or she will not comply with parental requests (e.g., to stay in or near the home or to check in regularly with the caregivers when in the community unsupervised), it is important to explore this problem with the caregiver. When caregivers report that their child or teenager leaves the home without permission (or without the caregiver's knowledge), it often indicates that further help is needed for this very important issue. For instance, the clinician may be able to elicit support from probation services (if involved with the youth), child welfare agencies or, if necessary, the local police, to help caregivers maintain their teenager's safety and ensure that either the teen is being supervised or that his or her whereabouts are being monitored by the caregiver or another appropriate adult.

It is particularly important to review the limits of confidentiality with adolescents at the outset of each session so that they understand that information given by them may be shared with their caregivers.

Child welfare

Considerations

Fire involvement by children and youth is a very serious matter. Some caregivers become highly alarmed and struggle to find appropriate ways to manage their child's fire involvement, particularly if it continues despite using their typical care-giving and disciplinary strategies. As a result, caregivers may respond to their child's fire involvement with inappropriate strategies. Some examples include the following:

1. harsh or abusive discipline in response to an episode of fire involvement by the child

2. threatening to use or using exposure to heat or fire; for example, forcibly touching a child's hand to a hot stove to "educate" a child regarding the dangers of firesetting and

3. locking a child with a history of fire involvement into his or her bedroom in order to manage night-time wandering or other behaviours. This child may have hidden fire-starting materials in the bedroom. If a fire were to start in the bedroom with the door locked, this child's ability to escape the fire would be compromised.

There is no evidence that these drastic strategies by caregivers are effective in eliminating fire involvement. There is, however, very good evidence that harsh discipline is counter-productive in stopping antisocial behaviour in general.

These types of caregiver responses usually require involvement of local child welfare authorities.

Other situations that may warrant consulting child welfare authorities include the following:

1. fire involvement that is targeted toward siblings

2. caregiver non-compliance with treatment recommendations, such as eliminating the child or youth's access to fire materials and/or unsupervised time in the community and

3. withdrawal from, or failure to attend, treatment.

Intervention modifications

Clinicians need to be proactive by preparing before becoming aware of such caregiver responses. This includes ensuring that caregivers and children are aware of the limits of confidentiality and knowing your child welfare reporting requirements.

In addition, it is helpful to become familiar with your local child welfare agencies so that, should these situations arise, you can respond in a routine, matter-of-fact way.

It is important for children's mental health and child welfare professionals to work collaboratively to ensure that the best interests of children and families are protected.

These measures should help to ensure that families continue to participate in your service in a meaningful and effective way.

References

Augimeri, L.K., Koegl, C.J. & Goldberg, K. (2001). Children under age 12 years who commit offenses: Canadian legal and treatment approaches. In R. Loeber and D.P. Farrington (Eds.), *Child Delinquents: Development, Interventions, and Service Needs* (Appendix B). Thousand Oaks, CA: Sage.

Augimeri, L.K., Koegl, C.J., Webster, C.D. & Levene, K.S. (2001). *Early Assessment Risk List for Boys (EARL-20B): Version 2.* Toronto: Earlscourt Child and Family Centre.

Bloomquist, M.L. & Schnell, S.V. (2002). *Helping Children with Aggression and Conduct Problems: Best Practices for Interventions.* New York: Guilford Press.

Cunningham, C.E., Bremner, R. & Boyle, M. (1995). Large group community-based parenting programs for families of preschoolers at risk for disruptive behaviour disorders: Utilization, cost effectiveness, and outcome. *Journal of Child Psychology and Psychiatry and Applied Disciplines, 36,* 1141–1159.

Dishion, T.J., McCord, J. & Poulin, F. (1999). When interventions harm: Peer groups and problem behavior. *American Psychologist, 54,* 755–764.

Earlscourt Child and Family Centre. (2001a). *SNAP™ Children's Group Manual.* Toronto: Earlscourt Child and Family Centre.

Earlscourt Child and Family Centre. (2001b). *SNAP™ Parent Group Manual.* Toronto: Earlscourt Child and Family Centre.

Gaynor, J. (1991). Firesetting. In M. Lewis (Ed.), *Child and Adolescent Psychiatry: A Comprehensive Textbook* (pp. 591–603). Baltimore: Williams & Wilkins.

Henggeler, S.W., Schoenwald, S.K., Borduin, C.M., Rowland, M.D. & Cunningham, P.B. (1998). *Multisystemic Treatment of Antisocial Behavior in Children and Adolescents.* New York: Guilford Press.

Hrynkiw-Augimeri, L., Pepler, D.D. & Goldberg K. (1993). An outreach program for children having police contact. *Canada's Mental Health, 41* (2), 7–12.

Kazdin, A.E., Siegel, T.C. & Bass, D. (1992). Cognitive problem-solving skills training and parent management training in the treatment of antisocial behavior in children. *Journal of Consulting and Clinical Psychology, 60,* 733–747.

Kazdin, A.E., Bass, D., Siegel, T.C. & Thomas, C. (1989). Cognitive-behavioral therapy and relationship therapy in the treatment of children referred for antisocial behavior. *Journal of Consulting and Clinical Psychology, 57,* 522–535.

Kendall, P.C. & Braswell, L. (1993). *Cognitive-Behavioral Therapy for Impulsive Children.* New York: Guilford Press.

Kolko, D.J. (2001). Efficacy of cognitive-behavioral treatment and fire safety education for children who set fires: Initial and follow-up outcomes. *Journal of Child Psychology and Psychiatry and Allied Disciplines, 42,* 359-369.

Kolko, D.J. (1996). Education and counseling for child firesetters: A comparison of skills training programs with standard practice. In E.D. Hibbs & P.S. Jensen (Eds.), *Psychosocial Treatments for Child and Adolescent Disorders: Empirically-Based Strategies for Clinical Practice* (pp. 409–433). Washington, D.C.: American Psychological Association.

Larson, J. & Lochman, J.E. (2002). *Helping School-Children Cope with Anger: A Cognitive-Behavioral Intervention.* New York: Guilford Press.

MacKay, S. & Henderson, J. (2002). *TAPP-C: Report to the Ministry of Public Safety and Security.* Toronto. Unpublished.

Reid, J.B., Patterson, G.R. & Snyder, J. (Eds.). (2002). *Antisocial Behavior in Children and Adolescents: A Developmental Analysis and Model for Intervention.* Washington, D.C.: American Psychological Association.

Shure, M.B. & Israeloff, R. (2000). *Raising a Thinking Preteen: The "I Can Problem Solve" Program for 8- to 12-Year-Olds*. New York: Henry Holt.

Webster, C.D., Augimeri, L.K. & Koegl, C.J. (2002). The under 12 outreach project for antisocial boys: A research-based clinical program. In R.R. Corrado, R. Roesch, S. Hart, and J.K. Gierowski (Eds.), *Multi-Problem Violent Youth: A Foundation for Comparative Research on Needs, Interventions and Outcomes* (pp. 207–218). Amsterdam: Ios Press.

Webster-Stratton, C. & Hancock, L. (1998). Training for parents of young children with conduct problems: Content, methods, and therapeutic processes. In J.M. Briesmeister and C.E. Schaefer (Eds.), *Handbook of Parent Training: Parents as Co-therapists for Children's Behavior Problems* (2nd ed.), (pp. 98–152). New York: John Wiley.

Webster-Stratton, C., Hollinsworth, T. & Kolpacoff, M. (1989). The long-term effectiveness and clinical significance of three cost-effective training programs for families with conduct-problem children. *Journal of Consulting and Clinical Psychology, 57,* 550–553.